BARRON'S PARENTING KEYS

KEYS TO PARENTING A CHILD WITH DOWN SYNDROME

Marlene Targ Brill, M.Ed.

BARRON'S

Cover photo by Scott Barrow, Inc., Cold Spring, NY

DEDICATION

To all the wonderful parents and children everywhere, especially my own, who inspired this book.

The author is grateful to Lucy Clocksin, Emily Kingsley, and Ann Jonaitis, for sharing their experiences and suggestions about raising a child who has disabilities. A special thank-you goes to Sue Mussatt, Direction Services of Illinois, Karin Melberg Schweir, Saskatchewan Association for Community Living, and George Smith, Special Olympics, for their assistance.

All inquiries should be addressed to:
Barron's Educational Series, Inc.
250 Wireless Boulevard
Hauppauge, NY 11788

Library of Congress Catalog Card No. 92-34282

International Standard Book No. 0-8120-1458-8

Library of Congress Cataloging-in-Publication Data

Brill, Marlene Targ.

Keys to parenting a child with Down syndrome   by Marlene Targ Brill.
  p. cm. – (Barron's parenting keys)

Includes index.

ISBN 0-8120-1458-8

1. Down's syndrome–Popular works. 2. Down's syndrome–Patients–Care. 3. Child rearing. 4. Down's syndrome–Patients–Family relationships. I. Title. II. Series.
RJ506.D68B75   1993
649'.1528–dc20   92-34282

                                                    CIP

PRINTED IN THE UNITED STATES OF AMERICA
3456 5500 987654321

CONTENTS

INTRODUCTION

No one plans to have a child with Down syndrome. In fact, most people take having a healthy baby for granted. Maybe your pregnancy went too smoothly to indicate otherwise, or you already have other children who were born without complications. Therefore, you were not prepared for the shock of hearing your newborn has Down syndrome. Few people are.

At first, Down syndrome may consume your life. The idea is so foreign to anything you planned. After a while, however, you will get past the surprise and confusion and the myriad other feelings. You'll realize there is a special little person who needs you and wants your love, just like any baby. Once you accept this baby as an individual, accepting Down syndrome becomes easier.

An important part of acceptance is understanding. You probably have many unanswered questions. You want to know what Down syndrome is and whether your child will experience unusual physical and learning problems. You worry about your child's future. These are concerns of every parent. Being a parent of a child who has Down syndrome intensifies the anxiety.

One bright spot is that you are seeking assistance at the best possible time in history. Years ago, parents of children with Down syndrome rarely received enough information about their child's condition. What they learned was riddled with misconceptions. Doctors gave little hope for their child's future. Usually, professionals encouraged parents to place their children in institutions. They assumed that all children with Down syndrome were too retarded to benefit society or lead fulfilling lives.

Thankfully, times have changed. Medical scientists developed cures to common illnesses experienced by many children with Down syndrome, thereby extending life spans by decades. Federal and state laws created the vehicle for early stimulation programs to give babies with Down syndrome a head start on learning. Regulations emphasized learning in traditional public schools with nondisabled children. Researchers documented studies that most children with Down syndrome may be retarded, but they have a wide range of capabilities if given the chance.

Once the condition was whispered about in secret. Now people with Down syndrome are on television shows and in commercials. Not every child will be a star, but neither will every nondisabled child. You need to discover what expectations are realistic for your child.

This book lays the foundation for understanding what Down syndrome means for you, your child, and your family. It has a broad, long-range perspective to give you an idea of handling today's challenges while preparing for tomorrow.

The content assumes you raise your child at home. If you have misgivings about handling a child with disabilities, try living with your child for a time, contacting some of the resources listed in this book for support, and applying suggestions given in the chapters. Whatever your final decision, at least you based it on reality rather than fear.

This book acknowledges feelings but keeps a positive tone. It reflects the hopes for all children with disabilities who are entering an age of greater acceptance and more opportunities. The can-do approach gives you the tools for action on your child's behalf.

Keys to Parenting a Child with Down Syndrome is organized in short, easy-to-read keys. The key format allows you to read sections applicable to your immediate situation quickly. Every key does not concern your child now. However, you may want to refer to the book as your child enters each new stage.

Part One, Understanding Down Syndrome, defines Down syndrome and presents current research into its causes. You will read about the most common myths surrounding the condition and learn why you are your child's most important advocate.

Part Two, Adjusting to a Child with Down Syndrome, discusses the range of feelings every family may experience upon learning the diagnosis. Key 7 addresses the uncomfortable topic of telling family and friends about the baby, and Keys 8 and 9 offer sources for emotional and informational support.

Balancing Family Relationships, Part Three, recognizes that Down syndrome touches everyone in the family—you, your child, and the other siblings. Because everyone is affected, feelings need to be recognized. This part offers suggestions for fostering a healthy emotional environment within the family.

Part Four, Your Child's Total Well-Being, deals with your child's health and how Down syndrome affects physical and mental development. Suggestions are offered for finding the right doctor and operating within the medical community more effectively.

In Part Five, Raising a Child with Down Syndrome, normal development is reviewed, so you can chart and encourage your child's progress. You receive concrete suggestions for managing behavior and organizing your child's world for success.

Your Child's Learning, Part Six, talks about the most recent legislation on children with disabilities. This section covers your child's rights to a functional education in the most mainstream setting, and it explains your role and rights as a parent or guardian. This part also provides an idea of the education process your child will follow and tips about how to help your child learn better.

Your Child's Future, Part Seven, discusses the nuts and bolts of preparing a child for leaving home. Alternatives for housing, employment, and financial planning are suggested. This section covers the sticky subject of sex education and reinforces the importance of peer relationships and recreational interests.

Questions and Answers near the end of the book contains answers to commonly asked questions and a quick overview of subjects covered in the book. There is also a glossary and lists of reading and organization resources that may be helpful in locating the best services for your child. Grandparents will find a special note devoted to them as well.

This book recognizes that legislation, trends, and acceptance of people with disabilities are changing at a rapid rate. I have heard this repeatedly from the many parents interviewed for this book. Therefore, the keys are designed to be a helpful place to start rather than a final source. I, and the parents who shared their feelings and contributed their recommendations, hope you find courage and understanding from reading this book and that you enjoy a happy, satisfying life with your new child.

Marlene Targ Brill, M.Ed.

1

~~~~~~

WHAT IS A BABY WITH DOWN SYNDROME LIKE?

Most parents wonder about their new child. What will the infant look like? What interests and talents will the baby develop? Now you wonder about Down syndrome.

Unless you know someone who has Down syndrome, you are probably unfamiliar with the term. Yet, you have been thrust into dealing with the disorder and making decisions for your baby. What you really need first are facts, and the best place to begin is by learning what Down syndrome is and what it implies.

Down syndrome is a condition that can affect any aspect of your baby's growth. The extent of its influence depends upon your child's makeup. At birth, babies with Down syndrome show a wide variety of mental abilities, behaviors, and physical development.

Certain characteristics will remain constant throughout your child's life. Others will improve with your loving guidance, appropriate medical attention, special early instruction, and continuing education. The important thing to remember is that children with Down syndrome have the same range of differences and capabilities as nondisabled children.

There are more than 50 signs of Down syndrome. All or even most of the traits rarely occur in the same person. Your child could have any combination of these characteristics at birth. This is how your doctor knew to investigate further. However, the most common signs involve physical characteristics and movement.

Poor Muscle Tone

Babies with Down syndrome may have poor muscle tone. Muscles are so relaxed that head and body parts flop. Arms and legs move too easily. Certain reflexes that require muscle tension are missing.

Poor muscle tone affects your baby's movement, strength, and general development. This is why it's important to begin muscle-strengthening exercises under the supervision of a trained therapist as soon as your baby is able. Regular exercise enhances muscle tone by firming muscles and increasing movement.

Head Features

Babies with Down syndrome have a distinct physical appearance. Sometimes the head is somewhat smaller than usual and the neck shorter. Loose folds of skin may be visible at the back of the neck after birth. Although all babies have soft head spots at birth, babies with Down syndrome have larger spots that may take longer to close. These skin folds and soft spots tend to disappear with age.

Facial Features

Most children with Down syndrome have eye openings that slant upward. Folds of skin called *epicanthal folds* cover the inner corners of both eyes. The iris of each eye may have white specks, called *Brushfield spots,* on the outer rim. These spots are barely noticeable and do not impair vision.

Other facial features tend to be slightly smaller than those of healthy children. Smaller noses with a flat bridge mean smaller nasal cavities, too. Therefore, your child may have a runny, congested nose more often. Some babies with Down syndrome are born with smaller mouths that have lowered upper portions. This makes the tongue appear larger. If your baby has poor muscle tone as well, she may have difficulty keeping her tongue inside the mouth.

Outer ears can be smaller, misshapen, or set lower on your baby's head. The smaller ear passages inside can be difficult to check for fluid and ear infections. Sometimes, pathways become blocked and cause hearing loss. Consequently, your infant needs an early hearing screening and regular follow-up tests.

Babies who have Down syndrome have their own patterns of developing teeth. Don't be surprised if some of your child's teeth refuse to erupt, are missing, or come in different sizes, shapes, or colors of enamel.

Hands and Feet

As your child grows, her hands and feet may be slightly smaller and stubbier than those of a nondisabled child. The fifth finger may curve inward, and there may be a space between the first and second toes. Fingerprints and footprints may be different because of the characteristic creases across the soles and palms. These features are barely visible, however, and do not affect development.

Overall Development

During the early months, your child will behave much like other infants. Unless there are unusual health problems, your baby will need the same care and attention as any baby. However, some infants with Down syndrome cry less often and sleep more. They may take longer to learn to suck from a nipple or roll over. They develop at a slower rate.

The question of mental development can be the most troubling for parents. At one time all children with Down syndrome were thought to be severely retarded. Gradually, studies showed that most of these children functioned within the mild to moderate range of retardation. Now few people in the know assume what a baby's future will be. Children with Down syndrome test within a wide range of mental abilities. For some, the potential is limitless.

Try not to let your child's earliest attempts at learning discourage you. They are unclear predictors of what is to come. As you will read in Key 21, early stimulation and quality education greatly improve your child's chances for a fulfilling life.

For now, enjoy your baby. She is more than a set of characteristics. First and foremost, she is a human being who needs your love.

2

~~~~~~

WHAT IS DOWN SYNDROME?

To understand Down syndrome, you need to know something about *human genetics*, the basic makeup of our bodies. All people have millions of cells in their bodies. Each cell carries an individual set of traits that determine growth, development, and physical characteristics, such as eye color, facial shape, and voice quality. These traits are regulated by message centers, called *genes*.

Genes are microscopic rods located in the parts of body cells called *chromosomes*. Usually there are 46 chromosomes in every human cell. These chromosomes are arranged in 23 pairs. Researchers have numbered each pair from 1 to 23 to study them more easily.

At conception, a baby's genes come from both parents. One chromosome of each pair is from the mother's egg, and the other chromosome of each pair is from the father's sperm. The pairs combine to help cells divide and multiply to produce a *fetus*, an unborn baby. (See Figure 1.) Sometimes, an accident in cell formation produces an extra chromosome. Fetuses with 47 chromosomes develop into babies who have Down syndrome.

Almost all (95 percent) children with Down syndrome have an extra cell in chromosome 21. This creates a triplet chromosome, rather than the usual pairs. Researchers refer to this type of chromosomal error as *trisomy 21*, meaning three chromosomes. (See Figure 2.)

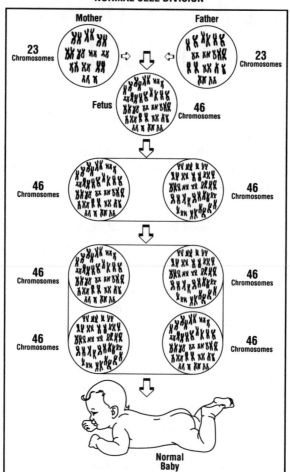

Figure 1.
NORMAL CELL DIVISION
Source: Public Health Service, Center for Disease Control, *Amniocentesis for Prenatal Chromosomal Diagnosis* (Atlanta: U.S. Department of Health and Human Services, 1980).

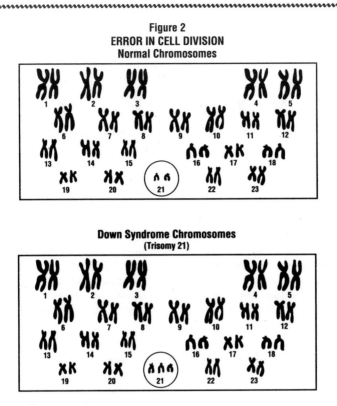

Figure 2
ERROR IN CELL DIVISION
Normal Chromosomes

Down Syndrome Chromosomes
(Trisomy 21)

Figure 2.
ERROR IN CELL DIVISION

Sources: National Down Syndrome Congress, *Down Syndrome* (Park Ridge, Illinois: National Down Syndrome Congress, 1988). Public Health Service, Center for Disease Control, *Amniocentesis for Prenatal Chromosomal Diagnosis* (Atlanta: U.S. Department of Health and Human Services, 1980). Karen Stray-Gundersen, *Babies with Down Syndrome, A New Parent's Guide* (Kensington, MD: Woodbine House, 1986).

Other forms of chromosomal errors are *translocation* and *mosaicism*. With translocation the child has 46 chromosomes, but one of the pair is broken. The broken part attaches—translocates—to another chromosome. In mosaicism some cells have 46 chromosomes and others have 47. Both translocation and mosaicism account for only four to five percent of all cases of Down syndrome. (See Figure 3.)

Figure 3
TRANSLOCATION DOWN SYNDROME

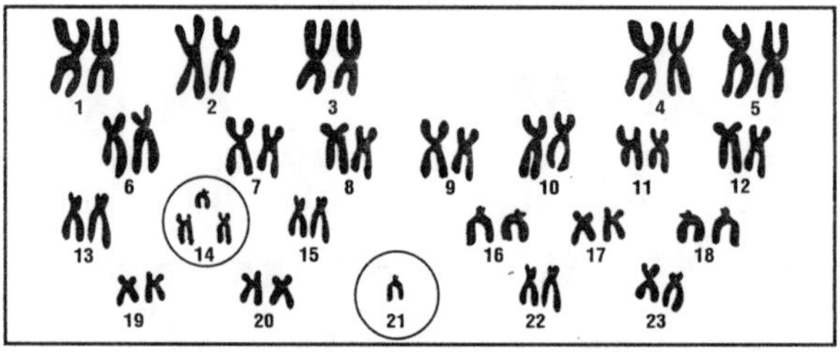

With this translocation, one of the two chromosomes 21 attached to chromosome 14.

Figure 3.

TRANSLOCATION DOWN SYNDROME

Sources: National Down Syndrome Congress, *Down Syndrome* (Park Ridge, Illinois: National Down Syndrome Congress, 1988). Public Health Service, Center for Disease Control, *Amniocentesis for Prenatal Chromosomal Diagnosis* (Atlanta: U.S. Department of Health and Human Services, 1980). Karen Stray-Gundersen, *Babies with Down Syndrome, A New Parent's Guide* (Kensington, MD: Woodbine House, 1986).

Before identifying Down syndrome, technicians take a blood sample from the baby. They place a small amount of blood in a petri dish to grow into a culture. Then they view a culture sampling under a high-powered microscope, which magnifies the cells enough to view chromosomal makeup. If there is an extra chromosome, the diagnosis is Down syndrome.

One extra chromosome is enough to interfere with orderly development of the body and brain. This is why your child may look and act differently from other children, be more prone to certain birth defects and subsequent illnesses, and mature more slowly. The extent of these problems varies with each child. Some children with Down syndrome are born healthy and with few characteristics. Others need immediate medical attention and close supervision for follow-up therapy. Your child with Down syndrome is unique.

3

WHAT CAUSES DOWN
SYNDROME?

The diagnosis is confirmed. Your child has Down syndrome. You ask why this had to happen to you and your baby. You naturally want to know where it came from and if you contributed to your child's condition.

Doctors describe Down syndrome as a genetic accident. They stress that there is nothing either parent did before or during pregnancy to cause the condition. Whatever you ate, drank, or felt at the time did not change your baby's genetic makeup. In other words, Down syndrome was not your fault!

Researchers have proposed many theories about the condition since British doctor J. Langdon Haydon Down first isolated and described Down's characteristics in 1866. Through the years, scientists have linked Down syndrome to hormonal imbalances, virus, parental alcoholism, vitamin deficiencies, potent drugs, or x-rays. None of these theories showed conclusive evidence about the primary cause of Down syndrome, however.

In 1959, Drs. Jerome Lejeune, Marthae Gauthier, and Raymond Turpin reported the first major breakthrough in identifying the origins of Down syndrome. Their research indicated that the condition resulted from an extra chromosome in every cell of the body. This discovery was an important step toward freeing parents from the guilt of

Figure 4
RELATIONSHIP BETWEEN DOWN SYNDROME
AND MOTHER'S AGE

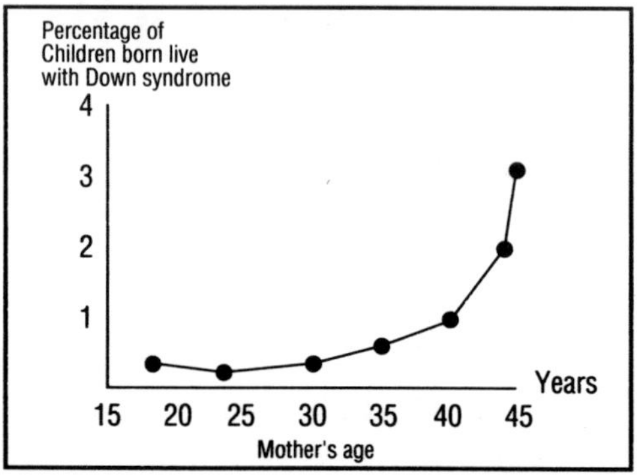

Figure 4.
RELATIONSHIP BETWEEN DOWN SYNDROME
AND MOTHER'S AGE
Source: National Down Syndrome Congress, *Down Syndrome* (Park Ridge, Illinois: National Down Syndrome Congress, 1988).

causing their child's Down syndrome. The doctors confirmed that genetic makeup was beyond parental control. Since their research, no new findings have definitively explained why certain cells divide improperly and result in Down syndrome. The exact cause and cure for Down syndrome remains a mystery.

Parental age is the only factor known to increase the risk of having a child with Down syndrome. The older the mother, the greater is the likelihood of having a baby with Down. The most significant increases occur after age 35. At this point, the chance of having a baby with Down syndrome is 1 in 400 births. By age 45, 1 in 35 live births results in Down syndrome. (See Figure 4.) Even with these telling numbers, 80 percent of the children with Down syndrome are born to mothers who are under age 35.

10

Researchers continue to investigate the correlation between father's age and frequency of Down syndrome. Estimates suggest that between 20 and 30 percent of the cases come from the father. Some studies connect the incidence of Down syndrome with the father's advancing age. Fathers older than 50 years have been shown to influence conception of a baby with Down syndrome.

Down syndrome is the most common chromosomal abnormality and leading genetic cause of mental retardation in the world. The condition affects every ethnic group, religion, and economic level. Each year about 4,000 children are born with Down syndrome in the United States. One baby with Down syndrome is born for every 800 to 1,000 births. The National Down Syndrome Society maintains that Down syndrome affects more than one-quarter million people in the United States.

Although many lives are touched by Down syndrome, significant research is relatively recent. High-powered microscopes and advanced technology have opened the door to exciting breakthroughs in genetics. Scientists are making great strides toward isolating and identifying genetic material on chromosome 21, which determines Down syndrome. Their hope is to uncover the relationship between Down syndrome and the development of intelligence and other physical traits. Once researchers understand what causes Down syndrome, they are sure that relief from related illnesses and, possibly, a cure will follow.

All this is for the future. For now, take one day at a time. Learn to care for your new baby. Discover how this wonderful little person—a person who happens to have Down syndrome—fits into your family.

4

~~~~~~

WHY BE INFORMED?

Parents are always getting advice—often without asking. As the parent of a child with disabilities, you may encounter even more people—doctors, therapists, teachers, and family and friends—who freely offer *their* ideas of what is best for *your* child. Most people mean well and consider their information reliable. Even in this age of enlightenment, however, many people have outdated or inaccurate facts. Their suggestions may differ from your goals for your child and family. To better evaluate what you hear and read, be informed.

Understand Your Child's Needs

Each stage in your child's development brings new challenges and new decisions. Your job is to understand how your child responds to these experiences and decide if they are appropriate. At first, you may be more concerned with your newborn's health and basic care. You want to know how to handle and interact with a baby who has disabilities. You are interested in your baby's eating, toileting, walking, and talking—everything any other parent considers.

As your baby matures, you think about social skills. You want your child to learn academics and practical skills for the future. After high school, your young adult will need help to make a smooth transition into the community. There will be work issues, living arrangements, and recreational programs to evaluate.

At each stage, children naturally take on more responsibility for decision making. However, your child with

Down syndrome may always need your guidance. To set priorities and make choices, you must know what options are available. You must decide which programs best suit your child's personality and skills at every stage. Your decisions affect your child's ability to be independent. You must stay informed.

Be Your Child's Advocate

A wise elementary school principal once told a hesitant parent, "Always be your child's advocate." Truer words were never spoken. You know your child best. You have the most investment in your child's success. You have the power to influence your child's future.

If you are uncomfortable with a doctor's diagnosis, get another opinion. If the school isn't serving your child's needs, ask questions. If therapy seems to be hurting rather than helping, request another evaluation. Trust your judgment.

Study and weigh all the options. Always recognize that you *do* have options. Be informed so you have the language and understanding to overcome intimidation by people who assume their professional titles give them the right to all decision making for your child.

Learn You Are Not Alone

Part of being informed is getting out into the community to learn about resources. During your information search, you will meet other parents who have a child with Down syndrome. You will find programs that deal with children who have comparable learning skills. You will discover support groups, play groups, professional organizations, many with large conferences, and university and hospital programs.

Besides offering information, these groups let you know that you are not alone. Other families are facing many of the same issues you are confronting. You can call these parents. You can get referrals from them. You can share everyday joys that only another parent in a similar situation can understand. Being informed makes sense for you, your child, and your family.

5

~~~~~~

MYTHS AND FACTS ABOUT DOWN SYNDROME

Your child with Down syndrome has many more opportunities now than decades ago. Recent legislation and emphasis on keeping children at home rather than placing them in institutions have led to greater understanding that people with Down syndrome can enjoy meaningful lives as part of the mainstream community. New educational, training, social, and work programs help boys and girls reach levels never dreamed of earlier. Yet, some people still harbor misconceptions about Down syndrome and the children who have it. Here are some of the most common myths you might encounter.

Myth: Children with Down syndrome make better progress living in institutions. Their needs far exceed what a family can provide at home.

Fact: For the past 20 years social service agencies have emphasized raising all children with handicaps at home. Many offer guidance and support services to increase a family's ability to cope with the demands of having a child who may need special care.

Since the trend began, researchers have documented that children who live with their families thrive beyond previous expectations. Conversely, they found that children failed to progress in institutions. When given the opportu-

nity, your child with Down syndrome will actively participate in your family and in community education, recreational, and social programs.

**Myth: Parents who raise their child with Down syn-
drome at home receive little community support.**

Fact: Federal laws on behalf of all people with disabilities
have created a new awareness of the need for basic support
services for families. Parents in almost every community
within the United States and Canada receive some health,
education, and recreational services for their disabled
children. You can find out more about what is available in
your area by contacting some of the organizations listed in
the Appendix under Resources.

**Myth: Since the doctor found only a few Down syn-
drome features, my baby will outgrow this condition.**

Fact: Down syndrome is a chromosomal error that is part
of your child's genetic makeup. The baby cannot outgrow
the condition. Your child either has the condition as
determined by blood tests, or your child does not. The
number of characteristics that are visible depends upon the
individual child.

**Myth: All children with Down syndrome have older
mothers.**

Fact: Most (80 percent) babies with Down syndrome are
born to women who are under 35 years. However, the
incidence of Down syndrome increases sharply with a
parent's age past 40. Although research suggests that
mothers play a slightly greater role in carrying Down
syndrome genes, the condition can come from either parent
at any age.

16

Myth: People with Down syndrome are always happy.

Fact: People with Down syndrome have the same range of feelings as the nonhandicapped population. They want to be happy, make friends, and feel they belong. Similarly, they are hurt, angry, or upset by unkind or thoughtless behavior.

Myth: Children with Down syndrome are severely retarded.

Fact: Most people with Down syndrome test within the mild to moderately retarded range. Some children achieve nearly normal intelligence; others are severely retarded. Previously, society had low expectations for children with Down syndrome. Communities provided little opportunity for children to show how capable they were. With higher expectations and better educational programs starting at younger ages, children with Down syndrome are making greater educational gains than ever thought possible. Those with severe retardation tend to have more severe medical complications.

Myth: Fewer Down's features means my baby will have greater intelligence.

Fact: Children with Down syndrome vary in the number and type of characteristic features they display. Your child can have any number of the possible 50 traits and still have Down syndrome. Each trait is independent, and the number bears no relation to your child's mental ability.

17

6

DEALING WITH YOUR FEELINGS

You decided to have a baby. You planned for the birth. You daydreamed about what your healthy baby would be like and how this new life would fit into your family. None of these visions included a diagnosis of Down syndrome. The news can be devastating!

Professionals and books like this can't tell you how to feel or for how long. They shouldn't. However, resources can offer some idea of the range of emotions experienced by others in the same situation. They can provide suggestions for helping yourself feel better.

Understanding Your Feelings

Don't be surprised to find yourself on a roller coaster of emotions, some so uncharacteristically extreme they are frightening. You may cry, scream, withdraw from everyone, or busy yourself with organizational details. You may be scared, angry, sad, or depressed or feel guilt, shame, or jealousy.

In the beginning, you may feel distant from your child. You worried about being a parent: now you worry how you will ever cope with raising a child with Down syndrome.

These are all normal responses. Everyone handles grief in their own way. Strong emotions may come and go for a long time. Feelings of "what if" may linger a lifetime. Allow yourself to have these reactions. They need to come out. As one parent said, "This is as bad as it gets."

The Grieving Process

Some parents found adjustment easier after they likened their child's diagnosis to a death in the family. The baby that died was the idealized baby of their dreams. They felt distant from their baby because the child wasn't the one they expected. Once the mourning process ended for their imaginary child, they began to build new dreams—dreams for the cuddly, loving baby who joined their family.

Although your emotional responses are unique, they may follow a sequence similar to what other parents have experienced. A common first reaction to a diagnosis of Down syndrome is utter shock. You are confused or frightened by the label placed on your small baby. You doubt the diagnosis. You question the doctors. You may remain detached from the baby, hoping that both the baby and the problems will go away if you don't become too attached. Denial takes over. After all, Down syndrome is something that happens only to other families.

As the shock subsides, an incredible sadness or grief may overwhelm you. You mourn the loss of the idealized baby you thought you knew during pregnancy.

Gradually, the sorrow turns into anger. "Why me?" you ask repeatedly. You may be embarrassed when you go out. You become jealous of parents who have healthy babies. You become angry when they don't appreciate how lucky they are.

Without enough accurate information your mind jumps from one stereotype to another. You fear raising a retarded child. You become frustrated with thoughtless and unresponsive medical personnel. You become angry with your family and friends, and even with your baby.

Little by little, your baby seduces you with smiles and coos as any baby does. You learn to feel joy in being part of

19

your child's small successes. The pain may reappear when you least expect it. For now, however, you begin to accept Down syndrome and you begin to enjoy the birth of your baby.

Helping the Process Along

Even during the most trying times, there are steps you can take to help yourself cope better.

- Give yourself permission to feel awful. Set aside time to be alone and to concentrate on whatever feelings emerge. Cry. Grieve. Think, even if for only ten minutes a day. A short time may be enough to revive your energy to face the stress of being a new parent—the parent of a child who seems so unfamiliar.

- Take time to make judgments carefully. If your baby requires medical attention, insist that physicians and other hospital staff explain your baby's condition and what the treatments entail. Then ask for some time to absorb the information before responding. Few decisions are so immediate that you can't have some time to collect your thoughts and be involved in the decision-making process.

- Don't overload your day. Concentrate on only the most important chores that need to be done. Let housework wait. Hold off on work outside the house. Give yourself the opportunity to sift through your emotions. You have been hurt deeply. You need time and nurturing to heal.

- Seek out other parents of children who have Down syndrome. They care about what you are going through because they have been there. They can give you the most believable encouragement because they know the successes they and their child have experienced. Parents who have lived through similar trying times can be a powerful source of reassurance. (See Key 8.)

20

- Remember that the baby has your genes, too. Right now you are getting used to the idea that your child has Down syndrome. However, you'll soon see that your child has many other traits unrelated to Downs. Maybe your child is good at drawing, has facility with languages, or excels in sports. You recognize the same talents in you or your spouse. Appreciating these skills may make it easier for you to accept that this is your child.
- Learn about Down syndrome. Facts help replace fear and inaction. Information makes you more comfortable with your child's condition. Armed with up-to-date facts, you can begin to make a long-range plan for your child and decide what is needed to get there. You learn that what you do will make a difference in your child's life. You become involved.

7

~~~~~~

DEALING WITH FAMILY, FRIENDS AND STRANGERS

S hould we tell others about the baby? When do we tell them? What do we say to the other children? These and other questions loom at a time when you are struggling with your own feelings.

Yet, people close to you, who care about your family, need to be told—and the sooner the better. You have nothing to hide or any reason to be ashamed.

Your initial contacts should be factual and candid. Your baby has Down syndrome. He may learn at a slower rate. For now, he may have certain medical problems, and most of these should be correctable. At this point, this is all you can say with certainty.

People may have a variety of reactions. Most are supportive. However, many people harbor outdated knowledge about Down syndrome, fears of any disability, or excessive pity for your situation. Here are some ways to help them and yourself:

- Call people before seeing them. One parent found this helpful for giving others an opportunity to adapt to the idea and deal with their own feelings.
- Offer pamphlets or books about Down syndrome for family and friends to read. Make sure the material is

accurate and current to dispel misconceptions or stereotypes that all children with Down syndrome are the same. You can purchase or copy print and nonprint materials from many of the resources listed at the end of this book.

- Think of jobs others can do for you. Some friends and relatives are concerned but feel helpless and uncomfortable about approaching you. One parent suggests telling friends and relatives to let her know if they find any information about Down syndrome. Others find it helpful for outsiders to take over routine chores needed to keep the home running. Friends and relatives can shop, take siblings for a visit, or cook a meal. Allow those close to you to help you through this crisis. You would do the same.

- Be honest about how you feel. Let people know when you need time to yourself. Tell them if you are feeling on edge or confused. By keeping lines of communication open, you are saying that you appreciate and want their support but for now you must have handle things in your own way.

- Trust your judgment. Make sure people understand that decisions about your baby are your own. Many well-meaning people, particularly grandparents, believe that their advice is gospel. You may hear that you should place the child in an institution or foster care or up for adoption. If your baby is unborn, someone may suggest you abort. Tell people you are considering all options and will make your own decisions, taking each day as it comes.

- Talk with the baby's sisters and brothers before they hear rumblings from people outside your family. Children are sensitive and want to be included in what goes on in the family.

How much siblings are told depends upon their level of understanding. Very young children merely need to be prepared for a new baby in the family. Older children require a matter-of-fact explanation that the baby has Down syndrome. Their brother will walk, talk, and learn but possibly more slowly than other children. He was born that way just as you were born like you are. Reassure siblings of your love, and leave the door open for more questions as they arise. They will. (See also Key 12.)

Grandparents may present more difficult problems. Because grandparents are so close to you, they may go through a grieving process similar to your own experience. The best way you can handle your parents is to be honest. Tell them you need their support and want them to feel comfortable with your child, but give them time to adjust. (See Special Note for Grandparents in the Appendix.)

- Let people get to know your baby. He will win them over just as he won you over. With time, they will understand that he is an individual who is more than Down syndrome.
- Accept that friends and priorities change. Some friends and family persist in weighing you down with old myths and stereotypes. If this happens, it is time to find new companions and a new support system, people who will help you cope better.

8

~~~~~~

PARENTS TALKING WITH OTHER PARENTS

Your baby is home and healthy or on the mend. Your strength is returning. You are ready to take control of your life and your baby's, but you are unsure about where to turn.

As mentioned earlier, a good place to begin is by contacting other parents who have children with Down syndrome. You may find that approaching one or two people at a time is much less intimidating than joining a group or seeking professional advice.

Support from other parents can be invaluable. Most parents of a child with disabilities offer an instant bond. They understand your hopes and fears. They know the challenges firsthand. They can suggest contacts to help you get through today while answering questions about what tomorrow might be like.

Contact the local National Down Syndrome Congress (NDSC), National Down Syndrome Society (NADS), United Way, Association for Retarded Citizens (ARC), or State Office of Developmental Disabilities for parent referrals. Information about national offices for these and other organizations is listed in Resources. Local numbers may be listed in your telephone directory, or your hospital social worker can provide them.

The National Information Center for Children and Youth with Disabilities (NICHCY) and the Family Resource Center on Disabilities provide local contacts for many areas where someone can give you the names of parents of children with disabilities. The community school district, hospital social worker, and pediatrician may also know parents who would be happy to talk with you.

These parents may invite you to join a parent group. As your baby grows and changes, your needs will change, too. A parent group can provide the information and emotional support to seek solutions to new challenges.

Historically, parent groups have played an important role in influencing treatment for people with disabilities. Parent groups lobbied government for laws and funding to give their children equal access to public programs. They organized schools and built sheltered living centers. More recently, they began training workshops to empower parents with the skills to advocate effectively for their children at every level.

Today, parents form influential organizations that function like any other special interest group. Lobbyists contact local government officials or speak with legislators in Washington, D.C. They stay informed through newsletters. They organize letter-writing campaigns. Members of grass-roots parent groups have learned the hard way that there is strength in numbers. You can benefit from their labor.

National organizations and the federal government sponsor formal parent groups, called Parent-To-Parent, Pilot Parents, Parents-Helping-Parents, or similar names. The NICHCY and Family Resource Center on Disabilities match parents like you with groups across the United States and in Canada.

Many parent groups hold meetings that invite professionals to speak. They have discussion groups and training sessions. Some prepare volunteers to visit new parents who recently received news about their infant. Many groups publish regular newsletters and sell pamphlets and books. They have the resources to help you and your family through each new stage of raising a child with disabilities. You can call to ask a question or attend meetings. You can become as involved as you want to be.

9

~~~~~~

SEEKING
PROFESSIONAL
SUPPORT

One minute you feel completely alone; another you are overwhelmed by the number of agencies and organizations that provide services and support. How do you make sense of the many resources that are available?

This key focuses on how to locate resources and explore options. As you find your way through the social service maze, you will gain confidence as a person, a parent, and your child's best advocate.

Organize Your Search

Locating services is a challenge, one that can be very frustrating. A way to reduce the stress of constantly seeking services for your child is to organize before you begin. The National Information Center for Children and Youth with Disabilities recommends the following process:

- Ask yourself these important questions before you contact anyone:

  1. What does your child need?
  2. What does your family need?
  3. What specific answers should result from my conversation or meeting? Do I need parent names, agency contacts, doctor or therapist referrals, or an

advocate to accompany me to an educational evaluation?

- Keep records of all your contacts. Write questions in a notebook before calling, and leave space for answers. Jot down the date and any notes from the contact. Record who you spoke with and who you were referred to in the same or other offices. People who were not helpful initially may be just the right contact in the future. Always ask the name and number of the person to whom you are being transferred in case you are disconnected.
- Organize records and files. Small children with disabilities create large piles of information. Store records in file folders, boxes or drawers, wherever is convenient. Separate medical and school files into logical categories before they become overwhelming. The reason to keep detailed records is that every specialist your child sees will ask about development and past experiences and treatment. Good record keeping allows you to recall details easily without relying on your memory.
- Develop a directory of local resources that will be handy for future questions.

Community Services

Community agencies are public and private organizations in the area that provide a variety of human services. They offer early intervention programs, speech therapy, physical therapy, occupational therapy, special education, recreation, modified housing, adaptive equipment, such as hearing aids, medical care, and counseling.

Many of these programs are administered by federal, county, or city governments and are funded by tax dollars. Therefore, the cost for services is minimal or nonexistent. State offices of education, recreation, housing, health, welfare, and advocacy can direct you to the nearest program for the assistance you need.

Private organizations offer a range of services either for a fee or on a sliding scale based on family income. Some of those concerned with disabilities are the Easter Seal Society and the March of Dimes. A network of services also exists through university-affiliated programs.

Where to Find Telephone Numbers
A good place to begin is with the contents of the local telephone directory. Many directories list community services in the front pages. Most separate listings for local, state, and federal government agencies. You can also look up a specific subject area, such as physicians or housing, in the buying guide subject index.

Another good resource is the school district. Some states fund school programs for children from birth through adult. In areas without resources the local school social worker or superintendent can help you locate agencies that provide services for your child.

The public library is another valuable resource. Librarians know which parenting and special education books and magazines list contacts as well as publish information. Make sure books about disability issues have copyrights after 1980. Older books may be outdated in terms of language, legislation, and research about what your child can accomplish.

Many hospitals make their social service, ombudspeople, and library departments available to parents who have medical questions. Nursing education departments also produce health education materials with understandable explanations. If you live near a university, contact the special education department or various subject libraries for information and referrals.

When You Can't Get Answers

If you exhausted all the resources you can find and still need answers, contact the local office of your elected representative. Local and state-level elected officials maintain staffs of people whose job is to answer voter questions.

You can find their office numbers in the telephone book or by calling information assistance. If you are unsure who the representative is, call the village or city administration office or the community or high school library.

Once you reach the representative's office, you must be prepared to ask specific questions and relate how often and from whom you tried to obtain answers and failed. You need to prove you made a thorough attempt on your own before legislators will step in on your behalf.

When You Live in a Remote or Rural Area

Many families who live in remote geographic areas have difficulty locating services. In some regions, officials claim that stretching limited resources for a few children is not cost effective. Too few children to provide state and federally mandated programs is no excuse to deny a child services, however.

If you have difficulty finding services because you are isolated geographically, there are agencies to contact that specialize in the concerns of rural families.

- The American Council on Rural Special Education (ACRES) is a national organization that improves services to individuals with disabilities. ACRES hosts an annual national conference, offers computerized networking, and produces a quarterly newsletter and other publications.
- County extension agencies connected with universities have information about what is available in rural areas.

31

- The state department of education has a responsibility to provide needed assistance to all its citizens.

Be persistent. The worst someone can say is they don't have what you need. Then try elsewhere. Many families have had to invent creative ways to obtain assistance. Some communicated with professionals in distant areas by CB radio, computers, answering machine or videotapes. Eventually their determination paid off for their child. So will yours.

10

~~~~~~

MAKING EACH PERSON SPECIAL

C hildren naturally mean life-style changes, whether they are the first-born or an addition. Their basic care, demands, and personalities alter established patterns in the home. Everyone in your household probably expected changes and looked forward to them. However, nobody expected Down syndrome.

For many families, the shock of Down syndrome gradually fades. As time passes, each person acclimates to having a cuddly baby around the house. Yet, attention focused on the special child's health, stimulation, and therapy often leaves each family member, parents included, shouting, "What about me? I'm special, too!"

Balance Every Family Member's Needs

As a parent you set the tone for adjustment to a family member with Down syndrome. From the beginning, let everyone know this child is part of the family rather than the center of it. He will have the same rights as everyone else but the world won't revolve around him because he has Down syndrome. Help everyone understand that the baby's condition may present more demands, but these demands will be balanced with those of the rest of the family.

Enlist Everyone's Support

Raising a child with Down syndrome requires the resources of the entire family. Divide the work load. Give every member of the family a share they can handle, including your child with Down syndrome when he is old enough. By contributing, each person feels important and a special part of the family.

Show Them They Are Special

Each day find some way to let all family members know they are special. Compliment them on how they look, or tell them how well they accomplished a task. Offer a surprise hug, kiss, or treat just for being a special person. Let family members know when you need a hug, too.

Do Something for Yourself

You can't give to others if you are running on empty. Plan time to do something for yourself to renew your energies. Perform an activity unrelated to children and Down syndrome. Take up a hobby you always wanted to explore. Start walking every day. Complete unfinished projects, or clean out the closet. The important thing is to revitalize yourself.

Avoid the superparent trap, when you are so scheduled that you are without free time. Maintain a steady pace that leaves you enough energy to enjoy your family. Concentrate on only those activities that must get done. If you are a list maker, record everything you want to do in a day. Determine the priority of items in terms of timeliness and urgency. Let the rest go in favor of doing something for yourself.

Play Together

Set aside time each week for family activities. Make sure you, your spouse, and your children can enjoy each other's company without worrying about schedules, appointments, work, or homework. Allow each person to select an activity for the day. Fly a kite. Have a tickle session or pillow fight. Roughhouse. Ensure that everyone is included in the fun. Let everyone know they are special.

11

~~~~~~

YOU AND YOUR SPOUSE

E ven the strongest relationships may bend under the strain of a child born with problems. You and your spouse may have difficulty coming to terms with your child's limitations. You may still have sorrow over losing the child of your dreams. You naturally fear the unknown—your child's health and future and your finances to care for special needs. All these concerns multiply as you try to maintain a quality relationship.

These concerns are serious, but they don't have to erode the bond you've taken energy to establish. Many parents find they become closer by solving problems together. They draw strength from each other and discover the courage to tackle each new stage. The support they give one another provides them with the ability to handle whatever challenges they may encounter.

Still, you and your spouse may differ in how you handle your emotions. One of you may become more sensitive, the other uncommunicative. One may be totally immersed with your child, the other distant. At times, you reverse these reactions as you try to sort out your feelings and learn to cope with this unexpected boarder. These new and different feelings are hard to understand.

Couples who have shaky relationships may use Down syndrome as an excuse for blame or anger against each other. One partner may exploit the commitment to an unhealthy child as justification for never making the effort to talk to or spend time with the other. Different ideas of child management may add to the arguments. As tensions mount, minor disagreements build into major battles.

Before this happens, consider some preventive measures.

Find Time to Communicate

Schedule regular uninterrupted sessions to share ideas and talk about your feelings. Try to understand each other's viewpoint. Listen to the feelings behind what is said. Help each other discover ways to work through unresolved emotions. If you can't agree about something, work out a compromise that is acceptable to both parties. You've solved problems together before. You can resolve your differences and make decisions together again.

Plan Time to Have Fun Together

Raising a family can be stressful. Every parent of a young child complains they lack the time, energy, and money to go out. The time and energy commitment that parents of children with Down syndrome make to their child's doctor's appointments, therapists, and stimulation activities compound the stress.

You need to give yourself permission to relax and enjoy each other alone. Give yourselves the opportunity to talk about life outside children. If money is a problem, ask friends or relatives to watch your child. If you are short on time, juggle your busy schedule. Cancel another social engagement, leave evening paperwork at the office one night, or let the house stay disorderly another day. Your relationship is worth it.

Reclaim Your Social Life

For some people, withdrawal is a common reaction to stress and exhaustion. As soon as you can, try to regain your social life. Being with other people as a couple is a good way to neutralize the intensity of everything you are going through together.

Share Responsibilities

You decided to have a child together. Continue the partnership throughout parenthood. Make sure you are both involved in your child's care and activities. Balance these responsibilities with both partners' outside commitments. Sharing the load reduces resentment and martyrdom.

Monitor each of your feelings carefully when one of you agrees to quit work and stay home with the baby. The spouse at home may eventually resent the responsibility and long to get back to the office. The working parent may feel left out if the spouse devotes too much time to the child and too little to their relationship. Make sure you don't drift apart at a time when you need each other most.

If you both work outside the home, find a friend, relative, or paid sitter to take your baby to infant stimulation and practice exercises. Enlist the services of an older child to be a parent helper when you are home. When your child is older, arrange day-care, preferably in a mainstream setting, or consider afterschool or special friend programs through the local school district.

Examine Your Finances

Money problems arising from Down syndrome can strain a marriage. Seek answers to financial difficulties together rather than worry or fight.

If you are caught in a costly medical emergency, you have options. Request a second opinion for expensive medical procedures. Ask about less expensive alternatives. Seek a workable arrangement with your child's doctors, hospital, and therapists. You may be entitled to government subsidy through Medicare or Medicaid or as a Qualified Medicare Beneficiary (See Key 40.)

Should you need outside assistance, consult a financial planner. Arrange for a loan to cover medical expenses. Contact the Down Syndrome Congress, Association for Retarded Citizens, or United Way for additional resources. Don't let money issues corrode your relationship.

Consider Outside Counsel

If you notice an increase in quarrels between you, take them as a warning sign. Arrange an uninterrupted meeting when you both can examine the problem. Don't leave until you decide the best way to put your relationship back on track. If you can't explain or resolve your differences, talk with someone objective, such as a friend, marriage counselor, or psychologist.

Take One Step at a Time

Learn to take each day as it comes. To plan your child's entire lifetime when there are so many unknowns is frightening and stressful. Celebrate your child's small accomplishments together, but remember to enjoy each other alone.

12

~~~~~~

UNDERSTANDING SIBLING REACTIONS

How would you feel if your husband or wife suddenly came home with another spouse? Moreover, you were expected to welcome this person into the family, share your belongings, and offer unconditional love. This may sound unlikely, yet psychologists often compare the impact of a new baby on siblings to the arrival of another spouse.

Helping a child adjust to a new baby is a challenge for any parent. Your job may be more complicated. Your children may need to adapt to a brother or sister who requires more of the family's time and attention. The adjustment may be a lifelong process as the needs of all your children change.

Many children and young adults admit that having a sibling with Down syndrome has been a mixed blessing. On the positive side, the experience made them more sensitive and patient. They learned to appreciate the gifts they possess and to accept other people's differences. However, they also believed that they faced many emotional challenges other children never experienced.

Sibling Reactions
Children differ in their responses to a sibling with Down syndrome. Some children may not notice any differences beyond the fact that an intruder has entered their

lives. However, even the most understanding child may resent the constant involvement required for a sick baby.

Sibling rivalry and jealousy are common reactions to feeling left out. Some siblings respond by helping with the baby to gain their parent's approval. Others imitate the baby, such as by thumb sucking, bed-wetting, or pretending to be sick. They figure if certain behaviors work for their brother or sister, they can work for them, too.

Older children who resent feeling neglected or burdened with care of a sibling may act out or pick fights. They conclude that even negative attention is better than nothing. In contrast, some struggle to be the perfect child, trying to compensate for their sibling's limitations.

As siblings mature, many become more self-conscious or embarrassed about having a brother or sister who looks and acts differently. At a time when they strive to fit in, they are saddled with a person who may talk or act oddly. They become even more upset if neighborhood children taunt them or their sibling with "dummy" or "retard." Emotions are jumbled as they are bothered about feeling angry, embarrassed for their sibling, and guilty for not being disabled.

Any stage can cause fears in a nondisabled sibling. Most are secret fears that develop through misunderstanding. Sometimes, children fear that their parents do not love them as much as the child who has a disability.

Another common worry is that Down syndrome is contagious. Often children are afraid to ask parents whether it is catching for fear the parents will be even more upset. Even if the nondisabled child understands that the condition comes at birth, the concern intensifies anew if grades suddenly dip at school. Low grades become confirmation that they are becoming retarded after all.

Preventive Measures

Children take their cues about a new baby from their parents. If you are loving and caring toward your baby, your other children will learn to appreciate their sibling. If you set a tone that respects everyone's feelings, your children will be freer to express themselves in a healthy way and accept each other's individual diffences.

- Be a good listener. Let your children know you care what they think no matter how negative. Don't judge their feelings. Let them know it's okay to get angry.
- Make sure you listen to your child with Down syndrome, too. Parents often emphasize how ordinary the child is but refuse to acknowledge that he can also have differences and fears like any child.
- Keep your nondisabled children informed. Children feel tension in the home and want to understand what is happening. Provide simple, clear explanations that suit their level of maturity.
- Be alert to trouble signs, such as withdrawal, anger, pushing, embarrassment, or constant complaints.
- Let children resolve their own problems if they bicker for your attention. If fighting becomes dangerous, separate those involved for a cooling-off period.
- Spend time with each child separately, even if only for a five-minute talk. Express your love and interest in their activities.
- Share responsibilities for your baby. Bring siblings to the hospital or to therapy visits so they can understand and be involved in the baby's life. Encourage their questions to doctors and therapists.
- Continue family activities everyone enjoyed before the baby arrived.
- Keep expectations for nondisabled children realistic. You may think that, by comparison, "normal" means

free of problems. You may forget that healthy people have individual differences and problems, also.

- Share and switch responsibilities with your spouse so you both spend uninterrupted time with each child.
- Help your child learn to deal with negative comments from other children about a sibling with disabilities. Listen to complaints of being teased, and help your nondisabled child understand the feelings that result. Offer enough information about the baby's condition to share with friends who tease. Encourage your nondisabled children to invite their friends over, where they can see how the new sibling is like any other child.
- Encourage your child to feel comfortable about having a sibling who has disabilities. Offer to talk with your child's classmates about Down syndrome and to bring the baby to school. Share the baby's accomplishments so your nondisabled child can feel proud of progress.
- Role-play with a younger nondisabled child to identify feelings. Exchange family roles.
- Read and talk about stories concerning other boys and girls who have siblings with disabilities. Stories let children know that others have similar feelings, questions, and concerns.
- Reassure your older nondisabled children that they will not be responsible for their sibling as an adult.
- Find a support group for your nondisabled child. Local hospitals and social service agencies may have sibling groups in which nondisabled children discuss their concerns in a nonthreatening environment.

Like any sibling, your child with Down syndrome will annoy, anger, disturb, and embarrass brothers and sisters. This is part of being a sibling. With your encouragement, however, your children will learn to accept each other and establish bonds that last forever.

13

~~~~~~

RESPITE CARE

E very parent needs breaks from the demands of parenting. Yet, parents of children with disabilities often hesitate to contact someone to watch a family member who has a disability. Perhaps these parents worry that their child's disability poses an added imposition on friends. They may view sitters as incapable of handling a child with special needs. The answer to such dilemmas may be *respite care*.

Respite care is a service that gives families a rest, a respite, from caring for someone with a disability. The break can be as short as an hour to run errands or handle a crisis or as long as a few weeks for a family vacation. During this time, someone who understands the needs of children with disabilities provides care. With respite care, parents feel comfortable with the knowledge that their child is in competent hands.

Recognition of the need for respite care emerged during the 1970s, when legislation entitled individuals with disabilities to live in the least restrictive environment. Thousands of people left institutions to live with their families within the community. Soon professionals saw families crumble under the strain from constant long-term care of a family member. They discovered that even the slightest relief from continuous responsibility was enough to revive family members and renew relationships.

Respite care gained support at the federal level after passage of the *Children's Justice Act* (Public Law 99-401) in 1988 and its 1989 amendment, Public Law 101-127, the *Children with Disability Temporary Care Reauthorization Act*. This act authorized funding for states to develop and implement affordable respite care programs and crisis nurseries. Since then, money and resources have been a constant problem, so you might have to be persistent to find the respite care that's right for you.

Respite care is available in different formats, depending upon whether your child stays at home or goes elsewhere for care. In-home services can be provided by trained sitters or paid health care aides. These people can come into your home for a limited time while you are there so you can handle other responsibilities, or they can live with your child while the rest of the family goes away. Some organizations provide volunteer or paid companions to accompany your child to recreational activities.

At times, you may need care for your child with disabilities outside the home. Hospitals, nursing care residences, and residential facilities often open rooms for short-term placement. Your child can also live with another family or in foster care. For daytime care, various community agencies run day-care centers and camp programs. When community services are limited, parents relieve each other by forming cooperatives to exchange sitting hours for time to handle other responsibilities.

To locate respite care, start by talking with staff at your child's program or local school. Ask other parents, or contact local groups associated with Down syndrome and mental retardation. Some states offer home services programs to relieve families in stress. Request the National Information Center for Children and Youth with Disabilities *State Resource Sheet* for resources in your state or call the local or national Lekotek center. For federally funded subsidized programs, contact the Texas Respite Resource Network and Access to Respite Care and Help Projects.

In some areas, groups of retired individuals, Camp Fire Boys or Camp Fire Girls, Foster Grandparents, or Big Brother and Big Sister programs assist families with respite care. Nursing schools and babysitting, nursing, and hospice services all have staff trained to manage someone with specific medical needs.

Contact these sources whether you need them now or not. Your child with disabilities will be covered in case of a family emergency or an opportunity for spontaneous fun. The important thing is to be comfortable with your child's care. Then you, your spouse, and your children can relax and enjoy your time together.

14

SHOULD WE HAVE
ANOTHER CHILD?

Many parents agonize over the decision to have another child. They wonder if they can manage the extra work load. They consider the effects of a sibling on their child with disabilities. They also struggle with their greatest fear—the risk of bringing another baby with Down syndrome into the family.

Books and advice from friends and relatives provide some direction, but they cannot resolve these issues for you. The final decision is an extremely personal one between you and your spouse. However, there are factors you can weigh to help you make your decision.

How Will a New Baby Affect Our Family?

Most parents ask the same questions about choosing to have another baby, whether their child is handicapped or not. The difference in your situation is one of degree. The fact that your child has Down syndrome increases the amount of time, energy, and money you spend on stimulation and medical care. The real question then becomes, Do you have the additional emotional, physical, and financial resources to handle another child and still be fair to your first child?

Other parents of children with Down syndrome who have siblings can be very helpful to you at this time. Ask them how a new baby affected each of their children. Find out if the children play together and stimulate each other, thereby making your job easier. Inquire whether the family benefited from the self-confidence and balance a healthy child can bring.

Will Our Next Baby Have Down Syndrome?

The chances for another baby with Down syndrome depend on many factors: your age, your family history, and the type of Down syndrome your child has. A *geneticist*, a scientist trained in the study of human genetics, is the best person to help you sort out these risk factors.

If your child has trisomy 21, the most common form of Down syndrome, your age may increase the chance of having another child with Down. Generally, parents under 40 years have a 1 in 100 risk of producing another child with trisomy 21. The risk increases significantly for women over 35 and men over 50. (See Key 3.)

With a child who has translocation Down syndrome, a rarer form that has a strong hereditary component, the geneticist is particularly concerned with family origins. At-risk mothers reveal a 1 in 10 chance of producing another child with Down syndrome, and at-risk fathers produce 1 in 22 babies with translocation.

If you decide to conceive another child, there are ways to test for Down syndrome during pregnancy.

- *Amniocentesis* is a common medical procedure to test for abnormal chromosomes. With amniocentesis, the doctor inserts a needle through the abdomen into the uterus to draw amniotic fluid, the fluid that surrounds the fetus, for analysis. The procedure is usually done between weeks 16 and 18, and it carries a 1 in 200 danger of inducing a miscarriage.
- *Chorionic villus sampling (CVS)* is a newer technique for evaluating chromosomes between weeks 8 and 11. Dur-

ing this procedure, doctors insert a needle either through the vagina and cervix or through the abdomen. The needle removes cells from the developing *placenta*, the sac protecting the fetus, for evaluation.

The benefit of CVS is the ability to detect genetic disorders quickly and at an earlier time during pregnancy. If tests prove positive, the woman has the option of choosing a safer first-trimester abortion. CVS is risky, however, causing spontaneous abortion in up to 1 in 100 women. In addition, recent data reveal that the test may cause specific deformities in anywhere from 1 in 200 to 1 in 1,000 babies born to mothers who have the test.

Testing decisions are becoming easier because of safer blood tests. A new blood test administered at 15 to 22 weeks screens mothers at risk for conceiving a child with genetic disorders. The test measures a woman's blood for levels of two hormones from the placenta and for alpha-fetoprotein, a protein produced in the fetus's liver. Unusual levels of these substances indicate further testing, such as by amniocentesis, because the pregnancy may be at risk. The test is mainly a screening device for women under 35, although some physicians may offer it to older patients.

A similar blood test, called *Barts triple test*, is being tested in England. This test is conducted at 16 weeks of pregnancy, and it screens blood for elevated levels of three chemicals that may indicate Down syndrome. If chemicals are found, the woman is offered amniocentesis to confirm Down syndrome. Physicians claim that this method identifies younger women at risk and older women at low risk despite age without exposing them unnecessarily to the dangers of amniocentesis.

With all these advances, modern technology has complicated decisions to have children. Many parents who discover their unborn child has Down syndrome grapple with the painful decision about whether to seek an abortion.

Decisions about having children have always been momentous. To simplify your decision now, consider your entire family. Picture how each would react to the addition of another child, one probably without a disability.

15

WILL MY CHILD GROW HEALTHY?

T he first and most immediate concern of any parent is with a child's health. Maybe your child has had life-threatening treatments already. You've spent days or weeks with your baby in intensive care. Even if your child was born healthy, you worry that the genes that caused Down syndrome will bring other health-related problems later. Although there are no guarantees for anyone's health, improved medical treatments indicate that your child with Down syndrome could be as healthy as any child.

Not long ago, the simplest problem was life threatening. Many children with Down syndrome lived in institutions that offered substandard care, at best. Parents who kept their children at home often found uninformed doctors who restricted treatment for individuals thought to be too limited to benefit from society. Even with the best care, children died of complications that have since become treatable. One study cited that 25 years ago only 50 percent of the children with Down syndrome lived until the tenth birthday.

Today, the picture is considerably brighter. Medical technology provides treatments for almost every health problem a child with Down syndrome may have. Life-saving surgery rescues babies born with internal malformations. New drugs eliminate infections. With proper and timely medical attention, your child can live a full and healthy life.

Routine medical care is important for every child, but it is critical for yours. Down syndrome can present certain problems at birth. As your child grows into an adult, the extra chromosome may make her more susceptible to the diseases of old age at an earlier age. Therefore, your approach to health must be long-term.

Children with Down syndrome require the same immunizations and health care screening as other children. In addition, regular examinations from a physician who understands your child's condition ensure that correctable situations are remedied early and medical disorders associated with Down syndrome are treated *before* a problem develops.

Untreated or undetected health problems can interfere with development, especially during the younger, more formative years. For example, reduced hearing from infections means your baby can't hear language to learn to talk. Poor vision limits normal exploration and play. Certain problems of old age strike people with Down syndrome as young adults, interfering with their independence. A comprehensive program of preventive medicine gives your child the resources to reach her full potential.

Several clinics specialize in health care for children and adults with developmental disabilities. The American Academy of Pediatrics keeps a list of clinics in the United States and Canada that follow its schedule of examinations and immunizations for children with Down syndrome. (see Table 1).

Table 1
IMMUNIZATION AND EXAMINATION RECOMMENDATIONS*

Procedures	Age																				
	Months									Years											
	1	2	4	6	9	12	15	18	24	3	4	5	6	8	10	12	14	16	18	20+
Measurements																				
Height and Weight	✓	✓	✓	✓	✓	✓	✓	✓	✓	✓	✓	✓	✓	✓	✓	✓	✓	✓	✓	✓
Head Size	✓	✓	✓	✓	✓	✓														
Blood Pressure										✓	✓	✓	✓	✓	✓	✓	✓	✓	✓	✓
Sensory Screening—Vision/Hearing (as needed)																				
Developmental and Behavioral Assessment	✓	✓	✓	✓	✓	✓	✓	✓	✓	✓	✓	✓	✓	✓	✓	✓	✓	✓		
Physical Examination	✓	✓	✓	✓	✓	✓	✓	✓	✓	✓	✓	✓	✓	✓	✓	✓	✓	✓	✓	✓
Metabolic Screen: Thyroid, PKU, etc. (as needed)	✓																			
Blood Tests (as needed)					✓				✓					✓				✓		
Urinalysis (as needed)				✓					✓					✓				✓		
Neck X-ray										✓						✓				
Immunizations																				
Tuberculin						✓												✓		
DTP		✓	✓	✓				✓				✓								
Polio		✓	✓				✓					✓								
MMR						✓														
Tetanus-Diptheria																✓				
Dental														✓						

A national network of programs associated with universities and teaching hospitals also provides services for children with disabilities. You can obtain a listing of these programs from the American Association of University Affiliated Programs for Persons with Developmental Disabilities or the U.S. Department of Health and Human Services Office of Maternal and Child Health. If you receive public assistance, ask a case worker where to locate medical assistance for your child.

The local branches of the Association for Retarded Citizens, National Down Syndrome Congress, and National Down Syndrome Society are important resources for medical services as well as other social services mentioned in this book. Remember that continuous, quality health care is only a telephone call away.

16

WORKING WITH THE
MEDICAL COMMUNITY

I deally, you and your child's medical team are partners. You seek quality health care for your child. Your doctor, with nurses and technicians, offers medical attention that will cure or reduce discomfort and maintain your child's health. Everyone wants your child healthy.

You may sometimes encounter snags in this relationship, however. Complicated office procedures and seeming indifference interfere with health management. Stress mounts under the best of circumstances. When your child's health is concerned, the added pressures can be overwhelming. Here are some strategies to reduce stress and keep your parent-doctor relationships on track.

Treatment Coordination

Down syndrome may indicate certain health problems that require a variety of medical specialists and evaluations, possibly beginning at birth. High-technology hospital units can be scary, and trips back and forth to stay with sick babies can be exhausting. Often, life-and-death decisions are required when parents feel most vulnerable.

Some parents complain that a diagnosis of Down syndrome exposes their child to excessive probes and pokes, sometimes missing routine care. They view each specialist as mainly interested in his or her own narrow field.

To assist you through these trying times, choose a physician who is willing to help you understand procedures and coordinate treatment. One physician overseeing treatment focuses health care on your child's total well-being and avoids fragmentation of care.

Usually a *pediatrician* is the primary care physician interested in a child's overall development. Your pediatrician should see your child for regular examinations and have the resources to make specialist referrals if necessary.

Compatible Goals

Before making an appointment, ask a receptionist if the doctor sees children with disabilities. Ask about credentials, fees, and appointment policies. Consider talking with the physician, also. You and your spouse may want to make an appointment without your baby.

Look for a physician who is comfortable with your child and knowledgeable about Down syndrome. This person should have up-to-date attitudes to evaluate your child's progress. Moreover, the doctor must be willing to work as part of the medical team that sees your child.

Be prepared to go elsewhere if a doctor:

- offers advice based on outdated stereotypes
- is uncomfortable with questions
- refuses to explain procedures in plain terms
- is unable to say "I don't know" and refer you to someone who can.

If you go to a clinic, ask a case coordinator to recommend the type of doctor you want for your child.

Appointment Scheduling

There will be times when you feel your whole life is spent waiting for doctors and therapists. If the doctor is routinely late, remember to call ahead. Request the first appointment of the day or the first slot after lunch to reduce waiting time from patient backlog. If you go to a clinic, ask what time of day is slowest and call just before you leave home to learn of any emergencies that would delay your visit.

Some children need a series of procedures from different technicians. Group your appointments on one day, closely together in time. This way, you reduce travel time and limit the number of days and hours involved with medical concerns.

Impatience is part of being a child. Bring toys to keep your son or daughter occupied in waiting rooms. Make the time special by playing favorite games with your child. By keeping yourself busy, unforeseen delays will irritate you less. If you anticipate a long wait, pack snacks as well.

Return Calls

Try to avoid the agony of waiting for a doctor's telephone call. Some questions or test results can be answered by the nurse. If you must talk with the physician or technician, ask the receptionist what time the doctor usually returns calls. Many doctors wait until the end of the day or the evening to return nonemergency calls.

If you will be at another number or unavailable for a few hours, call the receptionist with this information. This way, you can still conduct your business without taking the doctor's time to try, and fail, to call you.

Preparation for Appointments

Prepare a list of questions to ask during your visit. Ask as many questions as you need to understand and make informed decision about your child's treatment plan. Never allow a doctor to intimidate you or cut you short. You are paying for these professional services.

Bring a pencil and paper to make notes about your visit. You may receive considerable information that is difficult to digest. Your child may divert your full attention. Don't expect yourself to remember everything.

If you are too distracted, ask if the nurse can take your child out of the office while you talk with the doctor. You can also ask the doctor for a consultation meeting or a time when you can talk on the telephone without interruption.

Physician Requests

Professionals complain about patients, too. Here are some suggestions to uphold your part of the parent-physician partnership:

- Keep the telephone free when you are expecting the doctor's call.
- Notify the doctor's office at least 24 hours in advance if you need to cancel appointments.
- Be on time for appointments.
- Bring current insurance forms for billing with each visit.
- Make copies of x-rays for your files. Many hospitals keep film for only 7 to 10 years. New doctors may need to see original x-rays to determine whether your child's condition has changed.
- Maintain copies of previous doctor's records. Some doctors charge for reproducing files or require written confirmation for each copy discharged. This service can take weeks. You have a right to these files for reproduction as needed.
- Be prepared to give the doctor facts about your child's condition. You are with this little person most. You know your child best. If you feel something is wrong, follow your intuition. Help professionals provide targeted services for your child.

17

BIRTH IRREGULARITIES

C hildren with Down syndrome have a greater than average chance of being born with certain irregularities. Your doctor probably checked for these at birth, but some symptoms can go unrecognized or may not appear for days, weeks, or even years. By learning to identify potential health hazards, you can help the doctor provide immediate care for your child.

Heart Disease

About one-third of the babies born with Down syndrome have heart defects. Defects can occur in one of the four chambers of the heart or in the walls separating these chambers. Sometimes, there is a hole in the wall between two chambers, or the chamber walls and valves pumping blood to and from the heart are malformed.

When blood flow slows or is too great, *heart failure* develops. Without a proper blood supply, certain body functions become sluggish. Some signs of heart problems include:

- poor feeding
- skin changes to a bluish color during feeding
- easily fatigued
- inability to tolerate temperature changes
- listless when awake
- labored breathing

Heart failure requires immediate attention because it can be life threatening. Without treatment, the condition could damage lungs and restrict circulation, which affects all organs of the body.

Doctors who suspect a heart problem perform a variety of tests. The least intrusive is listening to the heart with a stethoscope. A stethoscope can detect a *heart murmur*, an unusual heart sound, that may indicate a defect. To investigate further, your doctor may order an *electrocardiogram*, a recording of the electrical impulses of the heart, *ultrasound*, which shows a visual picture of the heart from sound waves, or x-rays. You will probably remain with your child for these procedures to keep her calm and still.

The most conclusive test is *cardiac catheterization*. This process allows doctors to see inside the heart by inserting a slender, flexible tube into a vein going to the heart. The technique can be painful and requires that your child be anesthetized, as for any surgical procedure. Your child will require your attention during recovery.

Based on test results, the doctor may recommend either medication or surgery, or both. Frequently, medication is given to prevent infection and help the heart work more easily until the baby is strong enough for surgery. Years ago, heart surgery was very dangerous and advised for only the most extreme circumstances. Today, medical advances make heart surgery a common procedure, and the risks are greatly reduced.

Still, some parents face tough decisions when their child's heart is severely damaged. They may risk losing a child on the operating table or facing years of repeated invasive testing. When quality of life is weighed against surgery and found threatened, some parents choose to enjoy the quality time they have left with their child. Fortunately, such choices are becoming rarer. With immediate treatment and careful follow-up, children with Down syndrome who have heart disease also have longer, more hopeful futures.

Gastrointestinal Tract Problems

The *gastrointestinal tract* is the path that food takes through the body. In about 12 percent of the children born with Down syndrome, this path can be blocked or malformed. The most common problems occur in the esophagus leading into the stomach, the small intestine, the large intestine, and the rectum.

You will know if your infant has a gastrointestinal problem within the first weeks. Your baby will have recurrent bouts of vomiting, severe constipation, or bloody stools. Once diagnosed, your doctor will want to perform surgery immediately to correct any malformation. Corrective surgery allows the baby's body to absorb the nutrients it needs to be healthy again.

Cataracts

In the nondisabled population, *cataracts* usually come with old age, yet a small percentage (three percent) of children with Down syndrome are born with cataracts. A cataract is a condition that causes a film to grow over the lens of the eye and cloud vision. If left untreated, cataracts can cause blindness. A simple operation removes the cataract. As soon as your child is old enough, glasses will be recommended to correct any vision lost from the cataract.

For unknown reasons, children with Down syndrome tend to have more vision problems. If your child brings objects very close to the face or squints to see more clearly, she may have a vision problem. The most common are those that many children acquire: *nearsightedness*, when the eye clearly discerns only close objects, *farsightedness*, when the eye clearly differentiates only objects that are far away, and *crossed eyes*, when one or both eyes look inward. Adults with Down syndrome are more prone to cataracts, whether or not the cataracts appeared during infancy.

All these conditions are correctable with glasses. Therefore, your child needs regular eye examinations beginning at an early age to ensure that poor vision does not prevent her from learning.

18

COMMON HEALTH
PROBLEMS

Λll children have their share of health problems.
However, children with Down syndrome seem more
prone to certain ailments.

Respiratory Infections

Respiratory infections are the most common problems
of childhood, especially for children who have smaller nasal
and ear passages. Years ago the most serious infections,
bronchitis and pneumonia, shortened the lives of many
children who had Down syndrome. Today, modern medica-
tions have severely reduced the risk from infections.

Ear infections are the most recurrent problems for
younger children. They are more troublesome when youngsters haven't begun to talk. Your child can have increased
wax or fluid buildup as result of infection without your
knowing. Watch for these signs of ear problems, and call
your physician immediately:

- tugging at the ears
- crying if ears are touched
- prolonged crying or excessive crankiness with a cold
- fever of above 99 degrees Fahrenheit taken rectally

Antibiotics clear most infections. Sometimes, a second
antibiotic is needed for stubborn bacteria. If your child gets
too many infections the doctor may suggest *ear tubes*.
These are inserted into the ear drum to allow fluid to drain

and the ear to unblock. Should your child continue to have repeated ear infections, have an *audiologist*, an ear specialist, test for hearing loss.

Thyroid Disorders

The *thyroid gland* produces hormones that are essential to the nervous system. Sometimes, the gland produces too much—*hyperthyroidism*—or too little—*hypothyroidism*—of these hormones. Among children who have Down syndrome, about 20 percent develop thyroid dysfunction, usually from decreased hormone supply. Without enough hormones, your child's body processes slow, causing reduced growth and ability to learn.

Your infant should have received a thyroid test at birth as part of a complete blood workup. Continue to have your child checked regularly for thyroid hormone levels in the blood. Meanwhile, be alert to the signs of thyroid deficiency:

Infants	*Older Children*
Seldom cries	Repeated sensitivity to cold
Sleeps more than normal	Dry, coarse skin
Strange, hoarse cry	Muscle cramps
Slow, awkward movements	Tires easily
Constipated	Unusually slow growth
Feeding difficulties	Early sexual maturation
	Weight gain

Medication is the usual treatment for thyroid disorder. With proper drugs and regular monitoring by a physician, your child will stay healthy.

Skeletal Instability

Because babies with Down syndrome have poor muscle tone and limp joints, they are more prone to unstable *vertebrae*, the bones of the spine. The fibrous tissue surrounding these bones, the *ligaments*, are too weak to hold the bones together. This is especially a problem with the top two vertebrae of the neck. The result is a condition known as *atlantoaxial instability.*

Atlantoaxial instability increases your child's risk of spinal injury from participating in activities that might stress the head or neck. Consequently, physicians recommend examination and x-ray of the upper spine by age five years to rule out the problem. Some suggest an x-ray as early as three years after your child is walking and is more active.

Should instability be detected, the doctor may recommend surgery. Surgery allows continued movement and development but fuses the unstable vertebrae. After surgery, your child is restricted from strenuous activities and followed carefully by the doctor. Children who have Down syndrome without atlantoaxial instability may participate in all sports.

Dental Hygiene

Down syndrome may mean more dental problems. Your baby's upper jaw may grow at a slower rate than the lower jaw, resulting in teeth that meet improperly. Poor alignment will cause your baby to have a harder time chewing and biting. The smaller jaw may crowd new teeth.

As your child matures, the real problem will be gum disease. Many studies cite a reduced level of tooth decay but higher frequency of gum disease among people with Down syndrome. If left unchecked, gum disease can cause tooth loss.

To avoid gum disease, begin a thorough oral hygiene program with your child early. Institute toothbrushing at least twice a day. Schedule regular visits to the dentist beginning at age three. And limit the amount of sweets in your child's diet.

Alzheimer Disease

Adults with Down syndrome age earlier than nondisabled adults. Moreover, they are more likely than the general population to develop *Alzheimer disease*, a disorder that causes a steady deterioration in brain function. Recent research documents that the same gene abnormality on chromosome 21 occurs in both conditions. Alzheimer symptoms may appear as early as age 30 in the Down syndrome population, compared with age 40 or 50 in the general population.

Early warnings of Alzheimer disease are memory loss, disorientation, and sluggishness. As the disease progresses, language is affected and confusion increases. Gradually, coordination and independence diminish. The threat of Alzheimers disease thus has an impact on the type of living and working arrangements you make for your child.

Research into treatments and cures promises to reduce the trauma of the disease. Studies showing changes shared by Down syndrome and Alzheimer disease are helping scientists understand both disorders better.

Weight Control

One myth states that all children who have Down syndrome become overweight. In fact, research documents that about 25 percent of children with the condition are obese. The tendency is there.

As an infant, your child's poor muscle tone makes eating tiring, so your baby eats less and gains weight more slowly. Within a few months, eating becomes more regular but your child's growth rate may still be delayed.

Your pediatrician should have a growth chart that can help you monitor the balance between weight gain and growth in height. If your child gains too much weight, check the family diet for fats and sweets. Make sure you are not rewarding your child excessively with food, especially the kind that causes weight gain.

Another cause of weight gain is inactivity. Children with low muscle tone tend to move less because they must work harder. Create opportunities for your child to exercise more. Structure regular exercise sessions that are fun. Send an older child outside to play more often. Use games and playtime with you as rewards instead of food treats. Limit the time watching television, as you do for your other children. Exercise strengthens muscles, improves coordination, and enhances a positive self-image. Dispel the image that all children with Down syndrome are fat and sluggish.

19

~~~~~~

MENTAL DEVELOPMENT

Most children with Down syndrome have some degree of mental retardation. For unknown reasons, the same gene that causes Down syndrome changes how the brain develops. However, mental potential varies tremendously with each person. Therefore, no one can predict, or limit, the future achievements of your child.

Historically, professionals underestimated the mental capabilities associated with Down syndrome. Few children received the educational and social opportunities to stimulate intellectual growth. Without stimulation, people who had Down syndrome lived up to the low expectations society set for them.

Current trends oppose isolating these children. Now parents provide loving homes and advocate for early intervention programs, improved special education, and increased social acceptance. With quality support, your child's potential for learning is enormous.

What Is Mental Retardation?

Mental retardation refers to a person's ability to process information more slowly than other people their age. Learning definitely takes place, but at a reduced rate. The slower the pace, the more difficulty your child has with reasoning, evaluating, remembering, and associating ideas. The best thing you can do is forget the timetable reserved for other children. Your child will do everything, only it may take longer.

How Is Intelligence Measured?

As a baby, your child's progress will be measured against *developmental scales*. These scales consider when your child reaches such milestones as rolling over and talking and adapting to the world by learning self-help and social skills. Overall scale scores give some indication of how a baby is developing compared with others of the same age. However, they cannot foresee how much your baby can learn in the future.

Schools measure intelligence by *standardized tests*, which assess how your child applies thinking skills to acquired knowledge through formal and informal education. An *intelligence quotient*, or *IQ*, is computed from the test scores and then compared with those of other people of the same age to determine a general mental age.

Many question the validity of IQ scores. In the past, schools relied solely on these tests for placing children into different classroom levels for regular and special education. Teachers made assumptions about what and how much a student could learn based on these test scores. Educators now realize that there are many reasons for a low IQ score, and it doesn't always mean a child is retarded.

The controversy escalated as governments and professional organizations changed which scores constituted each level. At the same time, greater opportunities for individuals with Down syndrome translated into higher test scores. Recent studies document higher scores and provide more realistic assessments of what people with Down syndrome can accomplish. Therefore, take care that you read the most current research.

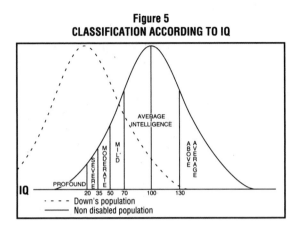

Figure 5
CLASSIFICATION ACCORDING TO IQ

Figure 5.
CLASSIFICATION ACCORDING TO IQ
Source: Data from Association for Retarded Citizens, Arlington, Texas, 1992.

As of 1992, the Association for Retarded Citizens cited four levels of retardation based on IQ: mild (IQ 51 to 70), moderate (IQ 36 to 50), severe (IQ 21 to 35), and profound (IQ under 20). To date, most people with Down syndrome function within the mild to moderate range, meaning they can learn the basics of reading, writing, and arithmetic and mature into semi-independent adults. Some children score within the low-average range. A few are severely retarded.

A range of intellectual functioning similar to that within the nondisabled population occurs with Down syndrome. If you think of the spread of intelligence as a bell curve (Figure 5), you notice that individuals with Down syndrome span the same distribution as individuals who are not disabled. The difference is that the entire curve for the Down's population is moved downward.

A true assessment of mental ability lies more in quality of life than an IQ score. Many children with Down syndrome learn to read and write, but many more gain independence and find a home within the community to live, work, and have a sense of accomplishment.

20

EARLY DEVELOPMENT

G rowing up is a continual interaction between the abilities a child is born with and the environment. Babies learn new skills by combining what comes naturally at a given age with what they learn from the world around them. Each new achievement is the basis for the next stage of learning. Simple skills become increasingly more difficult as children mature. This exciting growth and learning is called *development*. Your child with Down syndrome will develop this way, too.

All babies follow a similar sequence of development, yet there is a wide range of what is considered normal at each stage. Children differ in their inborn skills and how quickly they progress. One baby may say two words together at 14 months, and another might not talk until 20 months. Sometimes children skip a step altogether or take longer to advance to the next stage. They sit, stand, and walk without ever crawling. They scoot backward instead of crawling forward. These differences comprise a child's unique learning style.

Down syndrome can affect this range of normal maturation. The ability to recognize a normal progression gives you a more realistic picture of how your child functions. By understanding the stages of normal development, you will be better able to guide your baby from one step to the next. You learn to appreciate your child's learning style. You cannot control the developmental process, but you can intervene to ensure development progresses in a positive direction.

71

A Baby's World

Babies are born with the ability to learn, respond, and interact. At first, they concentrate on adjusting to life outside the womb. They listen for sounds and watch for eye contacts they find pleasurable. They are comforted by a soothing care giver. They begin a love affair with their parents based on gentle stroking, rocking, and quiet times talking and singing together.

As infants mature, they respond to people and objects around them and initiate interaction. They begin to understand facial expressions and voice tone and to respond with coos and smiles. They reach out to mobiles and toys and wiggle their little arms and legs with joy. This is a time for parents to talk and play with their baby even more. Through these exchanges, babies learn who they are, that they are loved and accepted, and that they can affect their world.

This growing self-awareness gives babies the confidence to reach out further, to explore more distant objects and discover people beyond themselves and their parents. Children now feel secure enough to rely on their skills separately from parents. They develop differentiated emotions. They seek independence with their parents' love, acceptance, and support.

Professionals generally categorize the developmental process into five basic areas besides physical growth: *sensorimotor, communication, cognition, social and emotional,* and *self-help.* You will hear these terms frequently. Resources and professionals you encounter apply them to the activities they recommend for your child.

Sensorimotor

Sensorimotor skills involve all large and small muscle movements and visual coordination of these motions. With

72

gross, or large, *motor development*, babies master body movements involving large muscles. The head and trunk develop first. As they gain control over the body, they lift their head and focus their eyes. Then they are ready to coordinate hand and eye movements and learn to sit, crawl, walk, and climb, all skills critical to exploring the world.

These large muscles develop before the small muscles in hands or feet. Gradually, *fine motor skills* unfold as babies acquire the movements necessary for detailed hand and finger projects. They master poking, pointing, and squeezing.

As eye movements coordinate with the hand movements, babies discover the joy of picking up tiny objects. This skill is called *eye-hand coordination*, and it is critical for learning to eat, dress, write, and care for themselves. Babies also explore the environment through other senses of taste, smell, sound, and touch.

Communication

Development of language is one of a child's most amazing accomplishments. Initial attempts at communication begin with cries. Crying is a way for babies to control their social environment.

As time goes on, babies cry less and practice more sounds. Babies around the world all utter the same grunts and coos. However, parents reinforce only those sounds that are part of their language. Gradually, these sounds turn into letter names, words, and sentences.

Educators talk about two ways of learning through communication. *Receptive language* is the facility to understand words, symbols, and gestures. *Expressive language* involves the ability to use these avenues to communicate with others. Most children understand more than they can communicate.

Cognition

Cognitive skills involve all the general information a child stores and processes. This includes the ability to think, reason, and solve problems. At first, babies respond in a very concrete way to basic needs. With time, they learn that objects exist even if they are out of sight. They understand the concepts of cause and effect and how objects and people relate to each other. They learn to use prior knowledge to solve daily challenges.

Social and Emotional

The ability to interact appropriately with other children and adults is important to any child's total well-being. Children develop the basis for self-esteem from these early relationships.

Young children want instant gratification. Reactions to displeasure are usually swift and extreme. As children mature, they develop patience. They become independent individuals who function appropriately within the community.

Self-Help

Self-help involves those activities of daily living that gradually become routine. In the beginning, babies are totally dependent on their care givers. As they grow, they assume responsibility for feeding, toothbrushing, bathing, toileting, and dressing.

Table 2 compares developmental milestones of children with and without Down syndrome. Try not to agonize over a particular task. Remember that these individual areas are part of a whole child. One area relates to another, and they all feed into your child's view of himself. In the end, this is what it's all about—raising a child who feels good about himself and what he accomplishes.

Table 2
COMPARATIVE DEVELOPMENTAL MILESTONES

Activity	Averages for Children with Down Syndrome (Age in Months)	Averages for Nondisabled Children (Age in Months)
Lifts head	1.5–3	1.0–2
Smiles and coos	1.0–3	0.5–3
Rolls over	2.0–12	2.0–10
Focuses on objects	2.0–3	2.0–4
Holds objects	3.0–4	3.0–7
Interest in sounds	3.0–7	3.0–9
Sits independently	6.0–17	4.0–8
Rhythmic vocalizations	5.0–10	5.0–7
Crawls	7.0–19	6.0–11
Finger-feeds	7.0–26	6.0–16
Speaks single words	9.0–30	7.0–14
Uses spoon	12.0–36	8.0–20
Walks	12.0–38	9.0–18
Solves simple problems	12.0–24	9.0–12
Speaks short sentences	16.0–44	13.0–30
Toileting	20.0–86	18.0–48
Dressing	28.0–70	20.0–42

Sources: Marlene Targ Brill, "Overview of Special Education" (Workshop for Title I Project, Chicago, 1979). Siegfried Pueschel, ed., *A Parent's Guide to Down Syndrome: Toward a Brighter Future.* (Baltimore: Brookes Publishing, 1990).

21

HOW WILL MY CHILD PROGRESS?

Watching a child grow and learn is a source of joy to any parent. The rewards of such accomplishments as walking, talking, and later independence in living and working are beyond words. As a parent of a child who has Down syndrome, you will experience these pleasures, also.

Your baby's genetic composition may create certain disabilities. Genes do not block a child from developing, however. The combination of your child's abilities and the particular environment she encounters will minimize obstacles to growth. In other words, the stimulation you provide your child from infancy until adulthood makes a difference.

An important part of this stimulation involves allowing your baby to explore. Some parents of a child with disabilities fall into the trap of being overprotective. They may have cared for their youngster through serious medical treatment. As health improved, they still treated the child as if she were sick and dependent. The child remains helpless thereafter.

Overprotectiveness interferes with development as much as any disability. Curb your desire to do everything for your baby. Instead, monitor your child's growth as you would any child's. Let her motivation be your guide.

Provide opportunities to stimulate natural curiosity and promote development. Encourage your child to explore and take risks.

Just like any child, her development may follow its own unique style. Don't be surprised if she has uneven progress in certain areas or misses others. The important thing is the quality of what she has learned. Can she walk steadily? Are her words understandable?

Sometimes, factors associated with Down syndrome interfere with your child's ability to progress smoothly. Your infant may take longer to reach established goals or seem to take forever to pass through a particular phase. Try not to be too frustrated. Concentrate on how your child is moving toward a reachable goal rather than how long it takes to get there.

If you understand Down syndrome and how it affects development, you can introduce new ways to overcome delays and challenges. Here are particular traits of Down syndrome to monitor and how they can influence your child's development.

Muscle Tone

Some variation in the quality and pattern of motor development is common among all children. Early attempts at coordination appear awkward and shaky. Therefore, parents of children with Down syndrome often have difficulty determining whether an irregularity is temporary or something lasting that requires attention.

Watch for signs of poor muscle tone, which slows your child's ability to master primary motor skills. When muscles are weak, your baby has difficulty lifting her head, grasping toys, or pulling herself to sitting and standing positions. Overly flexible joints create a challenge in gaining the stability to sit, crawl, and walk. Even feeding and language development can become sluggish because of the mouth, face, and upper torso muscles involved in eating and talking.

Fortunately, you can do something to improve your baby's muscle tone. Locate a good infant stimulation program that will evaluate your child's abilities. An early childhood specialist, speech pathologist, or physical therapist will teach you exercises you can do with your child at home. You may learn a new way of holding, touching, or talking with your baby or a method of rotating her body on the changing table, activities that will strengthen muscles and easily become part of your daily routine.

Hearing Loss

You already read that hearing loss is a major concern for children who have Down syndrome. More than 50 percent of these youngsters are born with or develop a mild hearing loss. When the problem becomes more severe, language development suffers. Without speech and language, social, cognitive, and self-help skills suffer. Make sure your child receives treatment from a physician before hearing loss develops.

Mental Retardation

With Down syndrome, there is always a possibility of mental retardation. Because retarded babies may be less responsive, interactions with them can be unrewarding. You may need to work harder to play and talk with your baby, if she seems unresponsive. Encourage siblings and grandparents to play with the baby, too. These interactions are vital to your child's sense of identity and belonging to the family. Over time, you will pick up subtle clues that indicate your baby wants to play and respond.

Do not assume your child can't learn because you notice mental retardation. Your child will progress, but at a slower pace. Studies indicate that children with Down syndrome have about 80 percent educability. Your baby will learn to sit, walk, talk, toilet train, take care of herself, read simple books, and more, only more slowly than average.

Mental retardation influences how your child develops cognitive skills. Learning remains at a concrete level longer, possibly forever. Your baby responds mainly to what she can see, touch, and hear. Her ability to learn from the environment is limited. Nondisabled children automatically pick up cues from their surroundings, but your baby needs specific instruction to learn basic skills. She also needs to practice these skills more often before she can master them, sometimes over and over again.

This means more planning from you. Creating a stimulating environment within your normal family routine is the most important way you can foster your child's development. The next thing you need is persistence. There will be plateaus that seem to drag on for weeks, but there will be major bursts of new learning, too. Trained educators and therapists can assist you in planning a program that will give you and your child pride in meeting each new challenge. As time goes on, you will adapt to your baby's pace. Seemingly small steps will become major accomplishments for your child and for you.

22

ORGANIZING FOR SUCCESS

Each day is a balancing act with any child. Your child's disability adds the extra therapy sessions, doctor visits, and formalized home practices straining the most even-tempered family-both mentally and physically. Here are some commonsense suggestions that may reduce the stresses of everyday child rearing.

Set Obtainable Goals for Your Child

Expectations give you and your family something to work toward. They provide a structure to hold onto when you are overburdened or encounter discouraging roadblocks.

Let your child's goals be guidelines rather than limitations. Be flexible enough to change goals as your child changes. Goals that are unrealistic or set too high or low can lead to frustration, for you and your child. Once your child can communicate, include him in the goal-setting process. Watching him attain realistic goals gives you hope, and they give your child self-confidence.

Arrange Your Baby's World

Every source you consult tells you to provide a variety of stimulation for your baby with Down syndrome. This can be a full-time job. Structure your child's environment to give him the stimulation he needs while allowing you freedom to attend to other responsibilities.

- Move your baby from room to room with you to change his surroundings. Have a bassinet, cradle, empty and cushioned drawer, or other safe place in every room where you spend large amounts of time.
- Talk to your baby as you go through your day together. With time, your voice may be enough to satisfy him should he need your attention.
- Carry your baby in a front or back pouch while you work.
- Draw a happy face on a large piece of cardboard and prop it on the side of his crib, baby seat, or stroller. Initially, babies focus on objects that have strong contrast, such as black-and-white drawings. By three to five months, they are attracted by bright colors, such as red and yellow.
- Use the car seat, stroller, or blanket on the floor to provide your baby with different views of his world.
- Attach mobiles, chimes, or musical toys to places where your baby lays or sits. Hang a bell near his door to let him know you are entering the room.
- Baby-proof the house as you would for any baby. (Call the local poison control center for details.) However, allow more time before replacing breakables and unpadding table corners. Your baby's weak muscles may contribute to unsteadiness and more accidents.

Organize Your Child's World for Growth

Arrange your home so your child can be as independent as possible.

- Move toys and clothing into reachable drawers and shelves.
- Install a hook in the coat closet that is low enough for your child to reach and hang up outerwear.
- Encourage independence by finding clothes that fit properly. Make sure clothes and shoes have fasteners

that can be mastered easily. If your child has difficulty buttoning, insert Velcro tabs.

- Allow your child choices about what to wear, but guide these choices so the items go together and are appropriate to the activity. If color matching is a problem, buy all clothes in the same favorite two or three coordinating colors.
- Develop a structured daily routine of washing, hair care, toothbrushing, and dressing that emphasizes good grooming and independent dressing. Give him a hairstyle that is easy to comb.
- Create a specific place for your child's possessions, and make sure he learns to replace them. Begin cleanup habits as soon as your child is mobile.
- Leave a stool in the bathroom so your child can reach the sink and toiletries.

Plan Ahead

Parents of young children learn early to expect the unexpected. Babies need food, toileting, bathing, and protection from a never-thought-possible physical feat at the most unforeseen time. Planning alternatives for such surprises reduces tension.

- Consider how much time it takes to perform an activity or leave the house, and allow an extra 15 minutes.
- Decide the night before what everyone should wear if choosing clothes is a problem. Select an extra outfit for your baby should he soil the first choice. Have your older child arrange his clothes so they are accessible in the morning.
- Pack your baby's bag with extra bottles and snacks should he get hungry off-schedule. Bring rattles, pacifiers, extra diapers, and a change of clothes.
- Bring a familiar toy, book, or activity to keep your child busy during long waiting times, such as for therapy or at

a restaurant. Always keep a small pad of paper and pencil for drawing or simple games, like connect-the-dot pictures, hangman, or connect-the-dot boxes.

- Prepare for bad days when you or your baby are out of sorts. Keep some new or favorite toys or games stashed away for such an occasion. Plop your child into the bathtub. Blow bubbles together, splash—anything relaxing. After your child is asleep, make time for a soothing bath for yourself.

Remember to Have Fun

One mother of a child with Down syndrome reminds us, "Not all of David is Down syndrome. The rest is little boy." If you find that all the time with your child concentrates on his Down syndrome—his therapy, home exercises and support groups—you are missing out on the joys of having a child. It's difficult, and unnatural, always to be planning purposeful activities. So remember the tickles, hugs, roughhousing, and hanging out together. Make time to relax, enjoy, and have fun with your child.

23

TIPS FOR MANAGING BEHAVIOR AND DISCIPLINE

Every child craves discipline, and your child is no different. She needs to know what is permitted within your family and community and what happens should she cross these boundaries.

When your child is young, the focus of managing behavior is on maintaining health and safety. As your child matures, expectations change. What was cute as a toddler is inappropriate for a school-age child or teenager. Now your child needs to learn positive ways to interact with other children and adults—to wait her turn, regulate her emotions, and understand she won't always have her way.

Some parents oppose disciplining their children. They view discipline as punishment rather than setting limits for happier, healthier children. However, think of what it would be like if none of us followed rules. Classrooms would have chaos. Jobs would never get done. We all need rules, and so does your child.

Sometimes, parents resist disciplining because the child has Down syndrome. They feel sorry for the child, or they feel guilty about the disability. They think someone who is retarded cannot learn how to behave.

Nothing could be further from the truth. Your child needs discipline to feel secure within her world. She wants to learn appropriate behavior. By knowing how to act, she gains greater independence and feels better about herself.

When you provide discipline, you are really offering a fairer, more loving way to live. Here are some suggestions for effective discipline.

Make Rules Fair

Devise family rules that are simple and understandable for your child's level of functioning. Above all, make sure they are fair. Let rules fit the situation, and set the same limits for every family member. Your child with Down syndrome wants to be part of the family and follow the same rules as your other children.

Be Consistent

Be firm about what is allowed and what isn't. If you flip-flop in your responses, your child will continue to try for the times when you allow the unacceptable. Your child with Down syndrome is like any child. She will test your limits—over and over again. Be consistent—it's the single most important thing you can do to help your child behave.

Be Positive

Very often children are unsure how to act. A subtle way to help your child learn is to praise, or reward, behaviors that you want repeated. Your positive response makes your child feel good about herself. Her feeling happier increases the likelihood of that behavior occurring again. Educators call this *positive reinforcement*. By concentrating on the positive, you focus on how well your child functions. As you delight in her success, you gain greater confidence as a parent.

Apply Behavior Modification Techniques

At times, your child will try your patience. Every child does. A way of changing how your child acts is to devise a behavior modification plan. *Behavior modification* is a strategy for molding actions with positive reinforcement. Maybe you want your child to stop making irritating sounds or to keep from pinching other children. Here are some tips for creating a behavior modification plan:

1. Decide what action or behavior is troublesome. Choose only one or two issues to work on at a time. This way, you can be more consistent and your child will have a greater chance to succeed without being confused or overwhelmed.

2. Identify how often and when the behavior occurs. You may see some patterns that give you insight into why your child acts a certain way.

3. Choose a reward, or positive reinforcer, that motivates your child. Babies like hugs, your smile and happy voice, or non-sugared cereal. Older children may need something more tangible, such as coins or stickers to collect and exchange for baseball cards or a release from unpleasant chores. Ask your child what she likes. Always remember that the goal is to phase out tangible rewards in favor of more social rewards, such as verbal praise. Eventually, your child will behave appropriately because it feels good.

4. Decide the time interval for presenting rewards. It can be immediately after completing a task, every half hour or at the end of the day. The timing depends upon your child's ability understand the connection between the reward and doing the right thing. In the beginning, reward closer to the desired behavior and more frequently. Verbally praise and reward your child. Say, "I like

the way you . . ." so she can understand which behavior deserves the reward.

5. Keep a chart on which your child can view her progress and evaluate whether the plan is working. At first, the undesirable behaviors may increase because your child is testing and learning the rules. Stick with your plan. After a couple of weeks, the behavior should subside. Then you can gradually reduce the number of times you reward your child and later switch from concrete rewards to hugs and kind words. If the plan isn't working, either change the reward or determine if you need to shorten the time frame so you can catch your child doing the right thing more frequently.

Some people are uncomfortable with the idea of behavior modification and positive reinforcement because they view them as bribery. We all work for rewards. We receive grades in school and salaries at work. We associate with people who think well of us and say so. Reinforcement is part of life.

Behavior modification is merely another tool for keeping your child and family on a positive track. It provides a nonthreatening, nonemotional, and organized plan for dealing with your child at a time when you may have reached your limit. Behavior modification helps you refocus on the positive and lets your child know that you like her—just not her specific behavior.

Ignore the Negative

Ignoring is a another technique for getting rid of undesirable behavior. Can you ever remember calling someone who never called you back? Pretty soon you stopped trying. The same happens with children. If you consistently ignore the same attention-getting behaviors, such as tantrums, teasing, or interrupting, they eventually stop.

Certain behavior is difficult to ignore. During these times, find something to busy yourself. If necessary, leave the room.

Time-Out

Some children have such disruptive behavior they are impossible to ignore. *Time-out*, when you calmly remove your child from the situation and place her in a safe place, gives you a reprieve and your child a chance to cool down. Use a timer to dictate the length of time-out, or allow your child to come out after the negative behavior stops. Make sure your child understands why she is in time-out, and suggest more appropriate behavior.

Set a Good Example

Be respectful of others. Create a considerate environment in your home. Behave as you want your child to behave. Her ability to live within the community depends in large part on her mastery of appropriate behavior.

24

YOUR CHILD'S RIGHT
TO EDUCATION—IT'S
THE LAW

Times are changing—but not fast enough. Governments can legislate equal access to education for all children. Researchers can agree that babies with disabilities profit from formal early instruction. However, funding programs and changing attitudes may take considerably longer. As the parent of a child with disabilities, you may have to initiate the education process and continue to advocate on your child's behalf.

An initial step toward helping your child through the education maze comes with understanding current laws and their jargon. These laws guarantee your child's rights to greater educational possibilities. Moreover, they ensure better preparation for a productive role in the community.

The Rehabilitation Act of 1973, Public Law 93-112, and the Americans with Disabilities Act of 1990, Public Law 101-336

The Rehabilitation Act of 1973 was one of the first public statements against discrimination of people with disabilities. Section 504 of the act particularly addresses your child's equal access to any schools receiving federal funds. The government withholds funding from education, vocational, and adult education programs, or places of employment that block opportunities for your child because of disabilities.

The Americans with Disabilities Act of 1990 extends the Rehabilitation Act by guaranteeing equal rights in employment, public accommodations, transportation, state and local government services, and telecommunications to people with disabilities. However, the implications of the law for your child are far-reaching and still open to interpretation at the local level. If you need more information or want to file a complaint, contact the U.S. Department of Justice, Civil Rights Division.

Education of the Handicapped Act, Public Law 94-142

Every child has the right to free public schooling. To guarantee the same right for your child with disabilities, Congress passed Public Law 94-142 in 1975. Under PL 94-142, states must provide the following:

- Schools must offer free appropriate public education to everyone between 3 and 21 years. By "appropriate," the law indicates that the learning situation must be suitable to your child's needs and at public expense, whether in a public or private setting. In addition, your child has the right to a curriculum that is functional and oriented to the future.
- Children with disabilities must receive education in the *least restrictive environment*, the setting most integrated with nonhandicapped children. Services may be offered in separate classes or schools *only* when your child's disability prevents satisfactory achievement within a regular situation. In areas where there are too few children with special needs, you may encounter such classes operated by a cooperative special education district that represents several school districts. Your

child's disability may be severe enough to require a more specialized setting, perhaps outside the district.

- Students must obtain related services as needed to enhance learning, such as speech, occupational or physical therapy, transportation, and counseling.
- Each child must receive an evaluation of specific needs for special education services. Any testing must be nondiscriminatory, and testers must adjust for any factors, such as hearing loss, that influence evaluation results. If another language besides English is spoken in the home, you can request that an interpreter be present at the district's expense or your child be tested by a psychologist who speaks your language.
- Children eligible for special education must receive services based on a written individualized education program (IEP) for school-age students or individualized family services plan (IFSP) for infants and toddlers. These plans state the type of special education, related services, and goals for various areas of development that pertain to your child.
- Individualized plans must be reviewed regularly and changed to adapt to your child's progress. A formal review meeting is required yearly, and full reevaluation should be conducted every three years.
- The rights of children with disabilities and their families are protected. The law guarantees that parents or guardians be part of the planning process for their child and that they can challenge any part of the plan they find incompatible with their child's goals.

Public Law 94-142 set standards for designating services to children with disabilities. However, the law upheld state practices that excluded public school services for children ages 3 to 5 and 18 to 21 and it left youths in many states hanging once they reached the cutoff age.

Education of the Handicapped Amendment of 1986, Public Law 99-457

The wealth of research confirming the effectiveness of special education for very young children resulted in passage of Public Law 99-457 in 1986. This law legislated early intervention and special education services for children from ages three to five who have handicaps. It also provided funds for states to serve children from birth through two years who are at risk for developing handicaps. Many states established child find programs to locate children who have developmental delays.

Individuals with Disabilities Education Act (IDEA), Public Law 101-476

This 1990 amendment to the Education of the Handicapped Act expanded and clarified important education services for children and youth with disabilities. The new legislation required states to provide programs for three to five year olds and to explore options for babies younger than three.

The amendment also mandated assistive devices at the government's expense for anyone who could benefit from their use. For older youths with disabilities, IDEA authorized a process for transition from school to adult community life. Schools are to plan for future schooling or employment, housing, recreation, and general adjustment to the community by a student's sixteenth birthday.

Each state interprets these law independently. To find out about the services in your district, contact the local school district, state education department, child find office, or health department. For more detailed written information about national legislation and your child's rights, contact the National Information Center for Handicapped Children and Youth.

~~~~~~

25

YOUR RIGHTS AS A PARENT

R evised special education laws are clear about parental involvement. You have specific rights and responsibilities to help make decisions about your child's education. Legislation authorizes your participation in judgments regarding your child's evaluation, program, and placement.

Some states view parental involvement as so vital that they provide training sessions to acquaint parents with the laws and familiarize them with the education process. Contact your state parent information and training project, the Family Resource Center on Disabilities, or the National Information Center for Children and Youth with Disabilities for information about sessions offered near you. Take advantage of your rights by being informed.

Right to Consent
Your consent is required before the local school district can administer any speech and hearing, psychological, developmental, educational, or neurologic tests. Once assessment has been made, your consent is integral to preparing and finalizing individualized programs for your child. You must agree in writing to initial placement and future changes. A signature on your child's individualized plan demonstrates your approval of the recommended education program.

Right to Participation

The law is well-defined about your right to participate in your child's education. One area spelled out in detail involves preparation of your child's individualized education program (IEP).

The local school district is required to notify you of the need for an IEP meeting and schedule it at a mutually agreed time. By law, meeting notices must indicate the purpose, time, location, and who will be present. Be sure to attend. If language is a problem, you can request or bring an interpreter.

The law intends parents to take an active role during planning meetings. You can join in discussions about your child's special education and related services. You can voice your concerns and education goals. You can decide with other participants which services the district will provide your child.

Equally important, the IEP meeting is a good opportunity to ask questions. Request explanations of anything you do not understand fully, especially terms and labels. Make sure that decisions are made based on more than a single test result.

Some parents feel more comfortable bringing an advocate to meetings. Preferably you want someone familiar with the laws and education system and with your child. Advocates can be supportive friends or neighbors, your child's independent evaluator or formal advocates from a local government agency or parent organization.

If no parent can attend, the district must find another method to ensure your participation, such as by conference call, individual telephone contact, or facsimile. After the meeting you should receive a written summary of the meeting for approval.

Right to Challenge Decisions

You have the right to disagree with any recommendations concerning your child's diagnosis, evaluation, services, and placement.

Ideally, you and district personnel can work out differences without seeking outside assistance. You can discuss your concerns informally with members of the IEP team or request another IEP meeting. District representatives must then respond in writing to your request.

In certain cases a trial period may be a compromise. You and the district agree to try an idea and to evaluate your child's progress after a prearranged time. Some school districts, however, prefer mediation by a third party. With mediation, you retain the right to state-level review.

If the district disagrees with you or refuses to act on repeated requests to meet, the law established a legal process you can follow to help your child. Procedures for appealing a decision are called *due process*. Due process entails your meeting with school representatives and an impartial hearing officer appointed by the state. The officer listens to both positions and prepares a final recommendation. Should you disagree with the recommendation, you can pursue legal action.

The entire process can be very involved, depending upon the state. If your petition for due process hearing concerns placement or services, your child will continue with the last agreed placement or service, unless you and the education team agree otherwise. Check with your state department of education for guidelines concerning the appeal of decisions and requests for due process hearings.

Right to Privacy

School districts keep a personal file on each student. Files include records of academic performance, health, behavior, test results, and communication regarding IEP meetings. You have a right to see these files, challenge their contents, and control access and release of information about your child.

The National Information Center for Children and Youth with Disabilities summarizes what the law says about your rights concerning school records:

- You can review educational records and copy them for your own files. Making a copy is important because school districts keep records only a short time after a student leaves.
- You have the right to request that school officials explain and interpret records.
- School officials may not destroy records if there is an outstanding request to inspect and review them.
- You may request changes in records thought to be inaccurate, misleading, or a violation of your child's rights. If school officials decide against changes, they must notify you in writing so you can request a due process hearing.
- Schools must keep track of requests for records by education or other social service agencies that are permitted by law to view student files. Verification of requests must be placed in your child's file and available for your review.

Massive legal changes in favor of individuals with disabilities and their families have taken place during the past three decades, yet laws guaranteeing educational rights are still evolving. For the most current federal and state legislation, contact your state department of education or the National Information Center for Children and Youth with Disabilities.

26

EVALUATION

The first step toward obtaining educational services for your child is to arrange for an evaluation, or assessment. *Evaluation* is the process of gathering information about your child's total development. Evaluation results are then used to determine what kind of assistance, if any, your child needs to progress.

Under the Individuals with Disabilities Act, states *must* assess children suspected of eligibility for special education at age three. Evaluations are at no cost to you. Some states fund evaluation to identify younger children and offer subsequent services for those at risk of having a disability. Since you are already aware of Down syndrome, your child's evaluation should focus on pinpointing his precise needs for progress at an optimum rate.

To request an evaluation, contact your local school principal or director of special education. If you seek infant assessment that is unavailable from your district, the principal can refer you to another medical or social service agency that can evaluate your baby's development.

Should the school refuse to test your preschooler or school-age child, you must receive a full explanation for the refusal in writing. Be sure to keep your copy of the letter. If you disagree, you may want to appeal the decision with the state office of special education.

Evaluation may also be requested by your physician, the school, or your child's teacher. In each case, you must give your permission in writing before evaluation can proceed.

The evaluation process involves gathering data from a variety of sources. Each state has procedures detailing who comprises the *multidisciplinary team* appraising your child's functional level. Federal law is clear about requiring your participation, however. Besides parental input, your child may see any combination of school psychologist, speech and language pathologist, physical therapist or adaptive physical education therapist, medical specialist, educational diagnostician, and classroom teacher.

These professionals observe your child and administer tests. They need to know how your child sees, hears, and moves. They want to examine every aspect of development, including intelligence, perceptual skills, social behavior, speech and language, academic ability, and vocational interests.

The law charges that special education placement may not be based on the results of a single test. Therefore, evaluators may administer more than one test to evaluate the same problem. The choice of tests is left to individual evaluators. The only requirement is that tests be nondiscriminatory, conducted in your primary language, and reasonable for the situation. If you want to learn about the most commonly administered tests, read the books by Wodrich and Bailey listed in the Appendix, Suggested Reading.

A case manager at the infant level or social worker from the school district will request certain information from you. You will be asked for records about medical history and reports from other professionals who worked with your child. Your observations about your child are important. The evaluation team wants to know about personality and how your child behaves in different situations. Sometimes, children perform for evaluators but not at home. At other times, the situation is reversed. These differences are important for the evaluator to document.

With very young children, functioning is assessed according to *developmental scales*, which measure at what age level your child performs a given task compared with standardized norms. Much of what these scales cover depends upon how your child responds at home. Therefore, your input is critical to the evaluation process.

Some programs or school districts provide their own evaluation team. All testing is then conducted within the school or district testing center. Smaller school districts, however may contract out services to private testers or other agencies, such as hospitals or health services.

A school representative should arrange the testing program at no cost to you. You have the right to question the credentials of any professional evaluating or working with your child. If you are unsatisfied for any reason, report back to the school district immediately.

Schedule only as many appointments together as your child can handle. You know best when he is tired and performing poorly. Your child may need more than one visit to the same professional for an accurate reading on performance. Seeing everyone involved and collecting reports can take from two to four weeks, or longer. Have patience with the evaluation process. Reliable, objective results are worth the inconvenience and wait.

27

~~~~~~

IFSP AND IEP

E ducators and government workers are notorious for their *acronyms*, words formed from the initials of the words in a phrase. For parents who have children with disabilities, acronyms only add to the confusion of acquiring and monitoring services for their child. The most common acronyms you will encounter as your child enters a program and progresses through the education system are IFSP (individual family service plan) and IEP (individual education program).

Individual Family Service Plan

After your baby is assessed and found eligible for early intervention services, you and the professional team will develop an individualized family service plan (IFSP). The IFSP is a written statement of all services indicated for your child. Areas examined for the IFSP are your child's physical, cognitive, speech and language, and social or self-help skills.

Preparation for the IFSP stems from the belief that your baby is best served by considering the needs of your entire family. Therefore, plan development concentrates on methods to support and enhance individual family strengths while giving your baby suitable assistance. For example, your child may receive physical or occupational therapy as indicated. However, treatment may occur at home or at a center, and you or a therapist, or both, will exercise your baby.

An IFSP is required by law for every child involved in an early intervention program that receives federal funds.

The law requires that the plan be reviewed at least every six months. You can request more frequent evaluation of your baby's progress.

Individualized Education Program

The individualized education program is similar to an IFSP, but it is for your school-age child with disabilities. The law requires an IEP meeting to develop a written education plan before your child can receive special education and related services. Written IEP documents serve as a vehicle to monitor your child's progress. The annual review meeting allows you to oversee whether your child actually receives the prescribed services. Since you will be involved in at least one IEP review session a year throughout your child's education, it is important that you understand and feel comfortable with the process.

The law establishes that the following people attend the special meeting with you to plan your child's education:

- your child's teacher
- a public school representative other than your child's teacher who is qualified to authorize or supervise your child's special education program
- your child, when appropriate
- any staff member who evaluated your child or has a current interest in your child's education program

The IEP meeting is a good opportunity for you to meet the key people affecting your child's educational future. Each person at the IEP meeting discusses your child's current performance. Specialists who evaluated your child explain which tests they administered and the outcome. Other teachers or therapists reveal how they view your child's behavior.

During the meeting you can ask questions, share your interpretations, and take notes. You will be asked how your child behaves outside school and how you view the progress. For example, if your child has low muscle tone that requires more physical and occupational therapy, say so. If speech is still garbled, request more intensive speech therapy. Sometimes, the IEP team needs to be reminded about services they may have overlooked. Such observations help everyone better understand your child's developmental needs.

From this discussion, the IEP team identifies your child's strengths and weaknesses. These qualities are matched with existing district resources, and the need for outside resources is determined.

The team then determines the content of your child's individualized education program. The final document includes the following information:

- a statement of your child's present education performance level
- annual educational goals and short-term instructional objectives for your child
- related support services, such as speech therapy or physical therapy, necessary to ensure that your child profits from the designated special education
- placement alternatives, indicating the most appropriate for your child. The IEP identifies such factors as activities, instructional setting and materials, and group size.
- projected initiation date and anticipated duration of services
- assistive devices or services your child needs to learn

To create the most fitting program for your child, you need to work closely with other IEP team members. Speak up. Disagree if you see the facts differently. Share your feelings about your child's education.

Sign the IEP only when you understand its contents, your questions have been answered, and you agree with the services, goals, and placements it lists. Remember, you always have other options. You can request another evaluation to reassess your child's progress, and you can request another review at any time. The important thing is to keep lines of communication open—for your child's sake.

28

EARLY INTERVENTION PROGRAMS

Many keys in this book stress the importance of early intervention for children with Down syndrome. This emphasis stems from a growing body of research documenting the significance of early learning for all children. More recent studies agree that the first three years of a child's life are crucial to later development. Moreover, many parents verify that structured programs for babies with Down syndrome significantly improved their child's later physical, mental, and social capabilities.

By enrolling your child in an early intervention program, you and your family benefit. Your child receives resources that tap a baby's natural desire to learn. The baby obtains the necessary treatment to minimize the effects of present or possible handicaps.

In turn, you find support at a time when your world seems shaky at best. Good early intervention can give you the skills to bolster your confidence as a parent of a child with special needs. Program staff can help you develop the kind of close, satisfying relationship experienced by any parent and child. They can help you plan realistic goals based on the successes you and your child have together.

Early intervention programs offer services that target infants and toddlers. They can begin as soon as your baby's health is assured and last until your child is three years old and ready for special education.

These services identify your baby's strengths and weaknesses and offer recommendations and follow-up. Services can be as uncomplicated as hearing tests or involved as physical, occupational, and speech therapy lasting months. The important thing is your child receives the needed attention when it can make the greatest impact—as early as possible.

Each state varies in the type of programs available. Unfortunately, there are significant differences in the quality and number of programs. You may have to be persistent until you find the best program for your child.

Ask other parents for referrals. Try to find programs with staff who are willing to work with your family on adjusting to a new baby, particularly one with special needs. Inquire whether the program has a variety of services. Visit different programs to compare how staff interacts with children and their parents. Ask specialists for credentials and whether they have experience with Down syndrome. Make sure the staff does not stereotype and limit your child because of Down syndrome. You want a place where your baby's unique qualities are valued.

In the past, early intervention focused on identifying weaknesses and devising activities to remediate these problems. Attention was on the child as client. Parents sometimes received exercises to do at home, but they were not considered part of the treatment team.

More recently, the program focus has become family centered. Many professionals realize that when family needs are satisfied, babies thrive. More programs now view parents as partners in their child's progress. Professionals work to bolster the parent-child relationship by teaching parents how to feel comfortable with their baby, practice activities at home, and enjoy the baby as part of the family.

At first, the early intervention team may visit your home to assess the family situation or observe family interaction at a center-based program site. Team members consider family life-style, other children, and daily routine in the treatment plan. They then help you integrate your child's recommended activities into the family routine.

Some programs lend parents toys, equipment, books, or audiovisual equipment. The staff may make additional home visits to ensure reasonable follow-up. Social workers help with insurance, child care, or parent support groups— whatever enhances family life.

Some of the professionals who may be involved in your child's early intervention program are discussed here. You may see one or more of these people in varying combinations.

Early childhood specialists, or infant educators, understand the development of very young children. They combine knowledge of normal development with information about how to proceed when development is not occurring as usual. They are interested in how your baby plays, responds to stimulation, and learns concepts. Early childhood specialists function as teachers, working with your baby and talking with you about progress.

Pediatric physical therapists help babies move better by improving bone, muscle, joint, and nerve function. With stretching and manipulating, your baby's body parts become stronger and more flexible. Therapists teach you strengthening exercises to incorporate into your baby's day.

Pediatric occupational therapists perform exercises similar to physical therapy. However, they focus on those physical skills that aid activities of daily living. They prescribe fine motor and sensory integration activities that emphasize shoulder, arm, and hand movements. With occupational therapy, you and your baby work on feeding, dressing, washing, and holding objects.

106

Speech and language therapists (or *pathologists*) assess hearing and devise activities to improve the use of mouth and face muscles for eating, sound production, and, eventually, communication. For babies who understand but are unable to produce recognizable words, many speech therapists teach manual signs to you and your toddler as part of traditional language development. Combining manual signs with spoken language is *total communication.* Signing helps you communicate with your child until speech becomes clearer. You can then phase out the signs. Studies show that total communication is an effective means of communication that does not inhibit eventual use of speech.

Social service personnel: social workers, mental health workers, and counselors are all titles for professionals who provide emotional support to families in stress. They may provide individual or family counseling, organize parent support groups, or recommend other agencies for assistance.

Case managers coordinate services for the child and explain growth in each area. They provide the coordinated link between home and the program. Usually, case managers are knowledgeable in early childhood education and can help parents locate other services within the community, including preschool programs for children aged three to five.

In addition, your child's program may have consultants or other part-time members. A *pediatric nurse* may be available to assist you with health-related issues that interfere with development. A *psychologist* may observe your child, conduct standardized tests or provide family support, and a *nutritionist* may assist you with dietary needs.

When you team up with these professionals to reinforce the home-program bond, your child benefits.

29

‍‍

TIPS TO ENCOURAGE YOUR BABY'S PROGRESS

A s a parent you are your child's first and most important teacher. Your playing, talking, and interacting have the greatest role in how your child develops. All the specialists your child may encounter can never replace this special relationship and intimate knowledge you have of your child. Every baby needs a loving and stimulating environment to thrive. You provide this with your soothing voice, rocking, gentle touch, and caring way you attend to her needs. Like most babies, yours feels safe in your loving home. When she feels secure and calm, your baby is more open to learning about her world.

Because your baby has Down syndrome, she may require extra assistance to make the most of her surroundings. You may need to plan consciously for the learning situations many parents take for granted.

There is no prescribed way to teach your infant, however. Do what naturally gives you and your baby pleasure. Here are some suggestions to help your baby and you make the most of your planned time together. (For specific activities, see Appendix, Activities to Promote Your Baby's Development.)

- Plan activity times for when you are both rested. Think about your baby's most alert time of day. Consider when you have other responsibilities. Tired, stressed people cannot enjoy themselves, let alone have a productive session. Similarly, stop the session or switch activities if you or your child seems anxious or tired. Learn your baby's activity limits. If you are to practice an exercise for 10 minutes each session, break up the time throughout the day rather than exhaust either of you. Don't feel compelled to teach during every free moment or every day.

- Choose a relaxed setting for activities. Select lighting, and possibly music, that is soothing. An excited baby is tense and unable to perform and attend to the task.

- Learn your baby's unique signals. All babies, even those with Down syndrome, provide clues to how they are feeling. Your baby will offer different cries or body movements to indicate a full diaper, hunger, or weariness. By recognizing these initial attempts to communicate, you give your baby the confidence to reach out further.

- Be as consistent as you reasonably can in your responses. React with the same smiles or claps to reward your baby's efforts. By being consistent, you make your child's world more orderly. She learns more easily when the environment is predictable.

- Imitate your baby. Imitation is the primary way all babies learn. By imitating your infant's beginning sounds and movements, you increase the potential they will occur again. As your baby matures, you will be able to demonstrate sounds and actions for her to imitate. Allow time for her to grasp the lesson. Demonstrate a second time. Act pleased with the slightest response. By repeating the activity, you can gradually shape her response to the one you expect.

- Prepare to repeat activities. Repetition gives your baby a chance to perfect and feel comfortable with what she learns. You may find repetition boring, however. Avoid the temptation to change activities unless your baby gives you cues that the time is right.

- Be persistent. One of the most difficult jobs for parents is to continue when nothing seems to be happening. You are normal for feeling frustrated at times. Stick with the activity. Another milestone is just around the corner to recharge your empty battery.

- Vary your child's experiences. Make learning into fun games and social experiences. Use everyday situations as times to increase your baby's general awareness. At home, help your child notice different sights, smells, sounds, and textures. Take your child on outings and walks to stores, playgrounds, or museums. Describe where you are going, and point out what you see there. For example, name vegetables at the grocery store and talk about their shape and color. Resist the temptation to buy expensive learning toys. Most babies are happier with pans, measuring spoons, balls, and empty food cartons.

- Be positive about teaching your child. Reward your baby for her work. Tell her how well she does. Give her hugs and kisses. However, your enthusiasm must be honest.

Sometimes, you won't feel like teaching your baby. Depending upon the severity of her handicap, you may have difficulty finding the emotional or physical strength for a work session. Take a break. Talk with someone, perhaps another parent, who will understand your feelings. Don't feel guilty that you need some time to renew yourself. Every parent does.

Playing with your child is supposed to be fun, not a chore. Watch your baby progress. Rejoice in her accomplishments, no matter how small. Help her develop a positive sense of her achievements and self-worth.

30

~~~~~~

PARENTS AND PROFESSIONALS AS PARTNERS

The updated laws intend you to be a full partner with the professionals who make decisions about your child's education. To do the best job, you and your child's professional team need to develop the type of relationship that allows ongoing give-and-take. When you work together everyone benefits, especially your child.

However, constructive parent-professional relationships can't be legislated. You must strive to acquire and foster this partnership. You must be able to advocate for your child without becoming the school's adversary. Here are some suggestions to support your child's learning and keep open the lines of communication with education professionals.

Prepare for Evaluations and Individual Educational Program (IEP) Meetings

There are several ways you can prepare for meetings with your child's education team. Being prepared gives you confidence and shows others you want to be part of the decision-making process.

- Review your child's records before the meeting. Reexamine previous reports. Request copies of any reports that might make your child's situation clearer. If you have questions about a test or report, contact the evaluator involved. Once you have reviewed the material, organize whatever you want to bring with you in a folder or envelope.

- Understand the laws and what is expected of you during initial and review meetings.
- Prepare a list of skills, interests, and special abilities your child exhibits at home. Be ready to talk about how your child behaves in different situations and any concerns you might want addressed by the education team. Use the Appendix, What Others Want to Know About Your Child, to help evaluate your child's achievements.
- Target realistic goals for your child. Think about your child's progress over the next few months and over the next year. Be prepared to suggest long- and short-term objectives you would like to see emphasized.
- Arrange any other materials you want to bring with you to the meeting. Do you have pencil and paper to take notes? Do you want to tape-record the meeting? Did you verify that tape recorders are acceptable to the rest of the team? Considerable information may be shared. Don't expect yourself to remember everything.
- Consult with your child, if appropriate, about what he would like to participate in or learn. Prepare a list together.

Plan Ways to Participate Actively in Your Child's Education

Some school systems are resistant to parent involvement other than PTA (Parent Teacher Association) fundraisers and signing report cards. You may have to be more assertive in reminding these professionals that you want to share responsibility for your child's education. The National Information Center for Children and Youth with Disabilities has several suggestions for initiating and maintaining good working relationships with school professionals.

- Tell your child's teachers and therapist that you are very interested in playing an active role in your child's educational program. At the early intervention level, this is obvious because you provide direct care for your baby. As your child matures, education and therapeutic service providers need to know they can call upon you for input as the person who knows your child best.

- Write a letter to a new teacher that discusses your child's capabilities and any behaviors being worked on at home and how. Use the opportunity to tell the teacher of your interest in supporting school efforts. Ask how the teacher prefers communications from home—by telephone, letter, reports, or visits?

- Ask for suggestions about what you can do to reinforce your child's school activities at home.

- Offer to explain any special devices, medication, or medical problem your child has. For example, teachers may be unfamiliar with the limitations placed on children with Down syndrome who have heart or spinal irregularities. Other students may think that information about your child's special computer or hearing aid is interesting.

- Tell teachers of any activities or significant events that may influence your child's performance or behavior at school. Request that teachers relate the same type of information to you to help you understand sudden changes in behavior at home.

- Request that samples of your child's work be sent home. If you have questions about the work or your child's progress, schedule an appointment with the teacher to discuss new strategies for meeting your child's goals. You child may need more immediate action than to wait until an official IEP meeting.

- Volunteer to help in the classroom or with school projects. When you are on-site you can see how the school operates and how your child interacts with other children and adults. If you work outside the home, lobby for nighttime meetings, assemblies, and activities when you can observe your child's school participation.
- Be considerate of team members' other responsibilities. Give teachers time to respond. If you find you are generating almost all the communications about your child, gently remind teachers of your concerns and ask how you can improve communication.

Let others know that your child's success and well-being at school are your primary interests. Be sure they understand that working together will help this occur.

31

~~~~~~

IS MAINSTREAMING RIGHT FOR MY CHILD?

S ociety expects children to become solid citizens who fit into the community mainstream, yet children with disabilities often have limited exposure to people and situations that will help them adjust to their surroundings as adults. The love and support your family provides cannot give your child all the experiences necessary to function independently outside the home. This comes with practice.

Educators finally realized that this practice should begin when a child first enters school, even preschool. After years of debate, professionals now believe that children with disabilities are best prepared for life if taught as much as possible within classrooms with their nondisabled peers. Educators call this *mainstreaming*, and you will hear the term often during your child's school career.

Some districts refer to mainstreaming as regular education initiative (REI), inclusive schooling, inclusion, or integrated classrooms. The meaning is the same. The idea is to foster greater autonomy in everyday settings. The concept evolved from legislation that called for the education of children with disabilities in the least restrictive environment. Although the least restrictive alternative does not guarantee education in regular education classes or imply that every child can benefit from mainstreaming, it supports these basic premises behind mainstreaming:

- Your child will be taught in a neighborhood school along with brothers and sisters, friends, and neighbors.
- Your child will learn in a setting with the same access to resources and events as peers without identified handicaps.
- Your child will receive an education in regular education classes whenever appropriate.

Mainstreaming can take different forms, depending upon your child's needs and the school district. Your child may spend the entire day in a regular nursery school or public school classroom or part of the day. A teacher assistant or therapist may support the regular education teacher by working with your child in the classroom or another room.

Some schools have *resource rooms*, separate classrooms with a special education teacher available for certain subjects or periods of the day. Some resource teachers spend part of the day with their students in the regular education classroom, providing support to students and teachers alike. Either the resource room or regular education classroom can be your child's homeroom.

Special education teachers are like regular education teachers, but they consider your child's total development. Your child will experience activities to promote self-help and social and physical growth in addition to academics.

Districts vary in their commitment to mainstreaming. You should understand some of the reasons for this in case you encounter resistance to mainstreaming your child.

- Some parents of children with disabilities worry that their child will lose needed services and specially trained teachers. They are concerned about their child's playmates.

- Some parents of children without disabilities worry that their child will learn less because children with disabilities require more teacher attention.
- Regular education teachers fear they will not have the skills to cope with disabilities.
- Administrators who support cooperative special education programs fear for their turf should all children be moved into regular classes.

The limited research to date contradicts most of these concerns. Studies indicate that children placed in regular education learn to talk more and socialize better. Follow-through with individual education program meetings ensures that valuable services are maintained when necessary.

Many districts have documented the value of mainstreaming for their regular education students and educators. Researchers found that mainstreaming reduces fears and changes biases. Everyone becomes more tolerant. Children with and without disabilities become friends. Teachers learn to ignore labels and promote respect for the individual differences of all students. By being exposed to children with disabilities, teachers discover there is no limit to how much these children can learn. Everyone in the district learns that all students, including those with disabilities, are people first.

Whatever situations you encounter, your first priority is your child. He may benefit from mainstreaming at the outset, he may benefit from waiting a few years to enter a regular class, or he may always profit from a special education class.

How do you know whether mainstreaming is right for your child? Here are some questions to ask yourself and your child's professional team:

- Is my child being considered as an individual or part of a set policy, such as inclusion for lunch and music only?
- Does the integrated setting provide opportunities to interact with nonhandicapped peers, especially on a social basis?
- Will students and teachers in the integrated class have preparation for a child with disabilities?
- How will my child be prepared for mainstreaming?
- Has my child been in the current setting long enough to adjust and for professionals to accurately recommend any change?
- Will my child have the opportunity to receive the special services she needs? How will they be coordinated with the mainstream education?
- Can I still be involved with my child's program?
- Does the mainstream teacher have preconceived notions about how much my child can achieve?
- Does the teacher have a sincere interest and willingness to work with my child and special service personnel?
- Does the mainstream teacher teach to individual differences for all students?
- Can my child benefit from an integrated setting? Mainstreaming for social reasons only should be carefully examined. A total lack of academic skills will more likely defeat the intended purpose. A child must blend into a classroom before the rest of the students will be accepting.
- Will my child be kept productively busy in the integrated setting?
- Will my child be more comfortable with other children who have the same developmental level or chronological age?
- Will my child be included in everyday activities that will let her know she is truly part of the mainstream, such as

class pictures, field trips, or a locker near the main-stream class?

Choosing the right program for your child can be complicated. Take your time. Study the options. Work with your child's professional team. Consider your child's needs at the time, and understand that they will change. By all means, consider the most mainstreamed options.

32

TIPS TO HELP YOUR CHILD LEARN

S ome parents of children with disabilities believe that once their child enters school, they can finally sit back. They will find relief from being the main service provider and running to separate early intervention, physical, speech, and occupational therapy programs. Now school will take care of ensuring their child's improvement.

To a certain extent this is true, but even the parents of healthy children are involved in their child's education. They oversee homework or review concepts that give their child trouble. Because your child may have developmental lags, you need to monitor your child's progress even more closely.

At home, this may mean continuing the formal and informal learning sessions that began when your child was a baby. Several suggestions from Key 29, Tips to Encourage Your Baby's Progress, apply to working with your school-age child as well. In addition, other tactics will ensure more productive periods with your older child.

Teach Tasks Step by Step

Decide what is important for your child to learn. Then, divide the task into understandable steps. Present each step in order, one at a time. Make sure your child can understand or perform each step before moving onto the next.

Test learning by having your child go back to the beginning and run through all the steps known so far. Pretty soon your child conquers the entire task.

Educators call this method *task analysis*, and it is applicable to most learning, from dressing skills to multiplication. You probably use task analysis unconsciously every day. When you start your car, you open the car door, slide inside, pull the car key from your pocket, hold the key in the correct direction, place the key into the ignition, and turn the key. You get the idea.

Your child may learn some tasks better backward, such as putting on socks. Place your child's sock almost completely pulled into place. Tell your child to pull on the sock. She practices the feeling of pulling the sock and knowing the correct position for the sock. Praise your child for completing the task. Then, pull the sock somewhat farther down your child's leg and repeat the command. Continue the same process with the sock placed lower and lower on your child's foot until it is completely off. With practice, your child will put on socks independently.

Apply General Laws of Learning

Certain principles pertain to every learning situation, whether formal or informal. By understanding these concepts, you can provide greater opportunities for your child's understanding:

- When two related events are presented at the same time and in the same place, they are learned together. A reward that follows immediately after a completed task reinforces both events. When you write *and* say a word, it is easier to remember.
- Repetition increases the chance that learning will occur. For example, your child will need frequent practice to learn rules or how to ask for goods at a store.

121

- Children tend to repeat acts that are satisfying; otherwise they lose interest. They repeat actions more often that are fun or result in praise, affection, money, or other rewards.
- Children learn more easily if the information presented together belongs together. For example, you remember meaningful words better than nonsense syllables or sequential words in a sentence more easily than scrambled words.

Provide Choices

Learning to choose teaches a child how to make decisions. When your child feels good about decision making, she becomes more confident and independent. Self-determination and confidence in decision making are part of the developmental process that begins in childhood.

Give your child structured choices as early as possible. Any child can make decisions affecting daily life, such as clothing choices, preferred activities, or chores to complete first. As your child matures, offer higher level decision-making responsibilities, such as selecting, buying, and preparing weekly lunches. Include your child in staff meetings whenever appropriate.

Use Clocks, Lists, and Charts Rather Than Threats and Shouts

Clocks, lists, and charts are unemotional, concrete ways to let your child know what is expected in terms of time and responsibilities. They offer structure and guidelines without parent nagging and overinvolvement.

Set the timer for how long your child is supposed to practice an activity or stay in time-out for misbehaving. If your child complains, tell her that the clock sets the rules, not you.

Prepare a chart or list that records all the activities or behaviors your child is responsible for during the day. (See Table 3.) Go through the list with your child at predetermined intervals every day. Place a check, star, or special sticker your child selects in the box for each completed activity. Make sure your child follows and understands her progress. Add responsibilities as your child can handle them.

Table 3
SAMPLE CHART: MY JOBS

Jobs	Mon.	Tues.	Wed.	Thurs.	Fri.	Sat.	Sun.
Wake up with alarm							
Dress							
Wash face and hands							
Brush teeth							
Comb hair							
Place pajamas in hamper							
Make bed							
Remove breakfast dishes							
Empty garbage							

Build Your Child's Self-confidence

One of the most important things you can do to motivate your child's learning is to help her develop a good self-image. You are already doing this by providing a secure home and varied experiences, by rewarding accomplishments, and by allowing her to handle choices and responsibility. Show your child you respect and value her as a person by the following actions:

- Knock on the door before entering her bedroom.
- Say "please" and "thank-you" just as you expect from her.
- Talk with her in private about any infractions, rather than in front of others.

123

- Introduce her to your friends and acquaintances.
- Include her in conversations.
- Give her the chance to respond without your prompting or answering on her behalf.
- Recognize her efforts, no matter how small.
- Listen carefully when she speaks by looking her in the eye to show your full attention.
- Say something positive to her each day.

When you give your child confidence, she feels good about herself and motivated to learn. Lessons in self-confidence begin at a young age, but their effects last a lifetime.

33

ASSISTIVE
TECHNOLOGY

T echnical advances are the wave of the future. Every day, companies develop new technologies and adapt others for daily living, particularly for education. Your child with Down syndrome needs to be included in the technology age, and it is up to you to understand its significance. Many of these advances can directly benefit your child with Down syndrome.

To assure your child's access to technology, the U.S. Congress passed the Technology-Related Assistance for Individuals with Disabilities Act of 1988, Public Law 100-407. The Tech Act, as it is commonly called, defines assistive technology as any item, equipment, or system that maintains or improves functioning for individuals with disabilities. The range of technology is broad, from hearing aids to computers. Because technology for individuals with disabilities changes so rapidly, the legislation funds activities to research and disseminate information to anyone dealing with disabilities. So you don't have to run out and buy the latest technological devices—just learn how to find assistance for your child (see Resources).

The best application of technology to reduce educational barriers related to Down syndrome is with computers. Some educators view computer-assisted education, especially for children with disabilities, as purely a fad. Others acknowledge that technology serves many valuable functions.

The National Down Syndrome Society entered the controversy by conducting a study. They found that children who participated in their Computer Education Project "experienced longer attention spans, increased self-esteem and skills and more positive interaction with siblings as a result of computer usage at home."

For thousands of captivated children with disabilities, computers open a whole new world of enjoyable recreation and learning. Computers are unemotional devices that are nonjudgmental. Users are in total control. Computers allow children to work independently and at their own rate. Moreover, children with disabilities learn to play games with children who are nondisabled. Computers provide an important bridge for social learning, especially in integrated classrooms.

Studies indicate that children with Down syndrome tend to learn visually. This means that your child may take in more information visually than aurally. Therefore, computers provide wonderful visual opportunities for learning and playing.

Computer manufacturers have teamed up with educators to devise adaptive equipment, specialized software programs, and unique classroom activities for children at varying levels of learning ability. The results are rapidly changing the way students are taught.

Voice synthesizers enable the computer to talk, and adapted screens attach to the front of the computer monitor for easier viewing. The combination of hearing and seeing sounds, words and sentences, and concepts helps many young children learn to talk and read. Children without language can also be assisted by talking and switching devices that allow them to communicate with the computer and other people. Adaptive keyboards, touch-sensitive screens, and power pads attached to keyboards provide very young children and those unable to operate conventional keyboards with easier ways to access programs.

Once children begin to learn, they practice reading, writing, and mathematics skills on computers. By the time they leave school, many teens with Down syndrome can operate computers well enough to handle data entry jobs and keep track of checking accounts. These young adults have the capacity to be more independent and productive.

Technology cannot cure the effects of Down syndrome, and computers may not be for your child, at least not for now. Still, you need to know what options are available for your child and what you can suggest to a school district that believes children with Down syndrome cannot profit as much from computer-assisted technology as other students. Computers can give your child another avenue for learning—an avenue that is becoming important to everyday functioning within the community.

34

~~~~~~

MAKING FRIENDS

You can teach your child skills. Your family can learn computers and sign language together. You can provide the best therapy and take your child to the best schools and programs. But all the technology and mainstream education cannot replace the joy of sharing free time with a special friend. Everyone needs friends to enrich their world, your child included.

Most of us take friends for granted. We tell a friend when we feel happy or sad. We go places with friends who like to do the same things we do. What about someone who has a disability?

People with disabilities usually have family who care about them. They know many people who are paid to work with them. Yet, they have few opportunities to be with someone outside the family who can be their friend.

One reason is that other children may feel uncomfortable with someone who may look or act differently. Children without disabilities may not realize that two people can be different and still have something in common. Another reason is that many nondisabled youngsters, even those in mainstreamed situations, have little contact with someone who has a disability.

Many parents say that one of their greatest heartbreaks is seeing their child with a disability left out of social situations. Isolation grows after the child leaves the educational system for community living. How can children be expected to mature socially and emotionally without satisfying peer interactions? How can they be truly mainstreamed if they are without community friends?

The time to start thinking about helping your child make friends is now. You can't force children to befriend your child, but you can create an atmosphere that helps your child and others feel more comfortable together.

Help Your Child Put the Best Foot Forward

How people look and act determines how others respond to them. Similarly, grooming and behavior reflect how individuals feel about themselves. Children with disabilities who call attention to themselves in a negative way appear less capable than they are. Their actions live up to these expectations, and others expect less from them. Therefore, you need to help your child fit in.

- Reward your child's appropriate social behaviors. At home, practice sharing and winning and losing graciously—skills that playmates need.
- Teach your child which actions are private, such as nose picking or scratching various body parts. Make sure your child goes on regular outings to practice public behavior.
- Watch out for any distracting behaviors, like rocking or making unusual sounds, and help your child eliminate them. (See Key 23.)
- Review situations that require good manners. Remind your child when to say, "please," "thank-you," and "excuse me" until it becomes automatic.
- Have your child carry tissues or a handkerchief. Make sure she knows to cover her mouth or turn her head away from others when sneezing or coughing.
- Help your child cope with teasing and name-calling. Let her know that all children get their share of teasing, and it hurts. Children tease because they feel uncomfortable

or bad about themselves. If your child can understand this, she may feel better.

- Choose hairstyles and clothes that are appropriate for your child's age.
- Teach your child to zip zippers, button buttons, and sew holes in clothing.

Arrange Social Situations

Provide opportunities for interaction with others of different ages and backgrounds. Through these situations, your child will gradually develop the social confidence to make friends independently.

- Let your neighbors meet your child and know you are a proud parent. Your enthusiasm will be a model for others to get to know and feel comfortable with your child.
- Invite neighborhood children to your home, for a walk or to the playground for planned activities. As they get to know your child, they might call on their own.
- Attend group parent-child play programs, such as those through the YMCA, YWCA, religious organizations, the local park district, government social service agencies, or community colleges.
- Leave your child with a sitter who cares for a number of children. Day-care homes are nice transitions to mainstreamed nursery school or larger day-care homes. Afterschool programs offer another chance for structured play.
- Organize your own play group, if you are unable to locate ongoing programs. Meet regularly so the children get to know one another. In some larger cities parent networks share the names of parents in the area to call, or you can contact your local Down syndrome organization for members who may be interested in forming a group with you.

- Suggest that your school-age child's classmates create a *circle of friends*, a concept begun in Canada. With this idea the teacher and class identify a mainstreamed child's strengths and determine what they can do to enhance these capabilities. Classmates take responsibility for ensuring that needs are met for the child. More important, they become the child's friend in a way that makes acceptance complete.

- Locate a local Best Buddies or similar program. *Best Buddies* is an organization that matches college students with teenagers and young adults who have mild to moderate mental retardation. The pair of buddies meets at least twice a month to do whatever the buddies choose—talk, go to movies, or play sports. The sole purpose is friendship.

The Best Buddies concept was developed in 1987 at Georgetown University by student Anthony Kennedy Shriver. Shriver believed Best Buddies was a way to use talent on campus to make a difference within the community. The program became so successful that now there are 111 chapters, with about 1,900 college members from more than 35 campuses.

To locate the nearest Best Buddies program, call the national office in Washington, D.C. or contact your local college or university. If your area lacks a program, you may want to start your own companion program. Make sure your child has a friend.

35

DEVELOPING
INTERESTS

L eisure is important to any child's life. The activities
accomplished during this time offer numerous benefits in a nonthreatening setting. By learning how to
spend free time in a fulfilling way, children discover how to
be happier with themselves and their playmates.

Most children, even many with Down syndrome, have
ideas about what they like to do. They reach out to
playmates, explore their world, and gain an understanding
of what interests satisfy them. However, your child may
need more direction in developing satisfying pastimes.

You may question the importance of dealing with this
portion of your child's life at a time when there is so much
else to consider. However, think about the fact that your
child averages between 55 and 75 hours of free time a week.
As an adult, your child may still have about 35 unplanned
hours each week. With such large numbers, interests
become more than luxuries for people with disabilities:
they are essential!

Your child will like to play with the same range of
things as other children. The difference is that you may
need to work harder to discover something that holds your
child's interest in a meaningful way. Offer experiences with
music, dressing up, art, crafts, books, and sports—all the
activities any child likes.

If you need assistance finding toys and activities for your child, contact the National Lekotek Center. Lekotek has centers around the world that support your efforts to help your child learn through play. You can spend time at the center with other families, or take materials and toys home on loan.

Lekotek also supports a technical network, Compuplay, for children with disabilities who are interested in computers. They offer drop-in sessions, classes, and summer camp to explore computer games.

Lasting interests often develop from classes and other formal activities. Many community agencies sponsor special programs for children with disabilities and programs accommodating all children.

- Libraries now have storytime and specific reading-for-fun programs.
- Park districts offer a sweeping range of classes, lessons, and team sports.
- Special education cooperatives pool their resources to administer recreational activities after school and on weekends.
- Museums and zoos of all kinds have tours, classes, and activities.
- Boy Scouts and Girl Scouts organize combined scouting groups with disabled and nondisabled children. Activities are adapted to individual capabilities.
- The Special Olympics provides individual and team sports training and athletic competition for children and adults with mental retardation. This international program offers an opportunity for people to compete in an adapted setting where everyone is a winner. The program began in 1968 after Eunice Kennedy Shriver decided that her campers with mental retardation were much more capable in physical activities than previous-

ly believed. The program expanded from Chicago to 50 states and more than 100 countries.

• Unified Sports is an outgrowth of the Special Olympics and the recent thrust toward mainstreamed activities for the disabled. With Unified Sports, people with mental retardation play on the same team as individuals without mental retardation who are similar in age and athletic ability. Contact the Special Olympics headquarters for Special Olympics and Unified Sports programs in your community.

Ask what your child enjoys doing. Cultivate these interests. Encourage a balance of activities, some that are social and some that are fun to do alone. Hobbies and interests are more than time fillers. They are vital for a healthy, fulfilling life-style.

36

~~~~~~

SEX EDUCATION

A dolescence is a time of excitement and confusion for all young people, those with and without Down syndrome. The teenage years signal an adolescent's passage from childhood into adulthood. With this transition come significant physical, mental, and emotional changes that result in sexual awakening.

Every parent has difficulty confronting their child's sexuality. Parents of children with disabilities may find they are particularly unsettled by their child's emerging social and sexual needs. In the past the tendency was to view individuals with Down syndrome as perennial children who are incapable of full sexual and social lives. However, your child will develop the same physical characteristics, sexual feelings, and desire for independence as any adolescent. You cannot inhibit this awakening any more than your child can.

Teenagers need to understand their sexuality so they can become responsible, independent adults. When you acknowledge and nurture this aspect of development, you prepare your adolescent for full emotional inclusion within the community.

The most valuable preparation you can offer is to provide accurate information about the body, love, sex, birth control, and sex-related diseases. Present the material in a simple, concrete, and matter-of-fact manner at a level your child can comprehend. Your child may be confused or take longer to understand bodily changes and their implications. With your patient guidance, however, your child will learn to feel comfortable with the complicated issues of sexuality and disability and the accompanying responsibilities.

If you are uneasy about these discussions, ask for assistance. Consult the resources in this book. Talk with your child's teachers, a counselor, parent support group, or Planned Parenthood. Obtain materials that are designed for individuals who understand differently.

Physical Changes

Studies of adolescent development indicate that children with Down syndrome mature at about the same rate as nondisabled youth. The first signs of physical changes can begin as early as the preteen years. This maturation introduces many new health and psychological concerns.

Adolescent girls benefit from clear discussion about menstruation *before* it occurs. Provide your daughter with information about the monthly cycles, breast development, and associated pubic hairs that are natural to becoming a woman. Give your daughter specific step-by-step training in how to care for herself during her periods. When she reaches 20, bring her to a gynecologist to begin regular pelvic examinations. Teach her to conduct a breast self-examination and the importance of a baseline mammogram at age 35.

Teenage boys experience striking physical changes as well. Your adolescent son needs to understand that wet dreams are as normal for boys as a crackling voice and facial and chest hairs. Help your son learn to deal with these variations and any teasing he might hear. Provide shaving instruction and directions for body care.

Sexuality

Sexual awareness is often puzzling to youths who may already have difficulty expressing themselves and understanding the subtle behaviors of others. You need to help your teenager cope with the confusing feelings involved with social relationships.

- Discuss what is private and public. For example, masturbation is normal for a child of any age, but the behavior is private. Additionally, your child's body parts are private and should not be exploited by anyone—friend, relative, or stranger.
- Instruct your child about acceptable ways to greet friends and strangers. Role-play several situations, such as meeting a stranger, date, or shopkeeper. Several resources are available to help you sort out appropriate social skills to emphasize, such as who can touch you, how, and where.
- Encourage your child's social activities. Some parents limit interaction in the hope that their child's sexual desires will lessen. The result is a youth who is denied essential physical and intellectual stimulation and parents who deny a basic part of their child's well-being.
- Decide how you and your adolescent feel about dating. Talk about what happens on a date. If your child goes on a date, should there be adult supervision? Who will provide transportation? What are behaviors for dating?
- Introduce your child to other adults with Down syndrome who have various relationships. Discuss what is involved in these relationships.

Birth Control

Society doesn't think of individuals with Down syndrome in terms of sex and marriage, yet many of these people are capable of deep, loving relationships. If people with disabilities are now living and working in the community, why not encourage emotional inclusion as well?

A long-term relationship may include sexual relations. Therefore, birth control becomes a sticky but important issue to address. Preliminary research cites that about 66 percent of males with Down syndrome produce sperm and 55 percent of females with Down syndrome ovulate. Adolescents who are expected to maintain independent and semi-independent lives within the community need to have instruction in birth control, parenting, and accountability in relationships.

Some parents may want to think about sterilization. Not long ago, females with Down syndrome who lived in institutions routinely received operations for sterilization. Today, most states prohibit involuntary sterilization unless your child is declared totally incompetent by the courts. Check with your local state's attorney and physician. Consider the least intrusive alternatives, and weigh the risks and benefits.

Be conscious of infringing on your child's rights to a full relationship. Your child with disabilities has the same desires that you have—to love and be loved, to share and to live in the same world as you do. Your child didn't ask to be born with Down syndrome, so don't restrict your child further by omitting this important aspect of life.

37

~~~~~~

TRANSITION PLANNING

All students eventually confront leaving secondary school. They follow a similar path to higher education or employment. However, traditional paths into the community have frequently been closed to youths in special education. Their families were left to plan for the future on their own. The task was overwhelming, with limited support services and agencies unclear about who was responsible for what.

More recently, legislators have acknowledged the difficulties of one family or agency trying to provide the experiences and resources to adequately assure youth with disabilities a productive life outside the home. In response, they created the Individuals with Disabilities Education Act (IDEA, Public Law 101-476). This law guarantees that a student's individualized education plan include a statement of transition services.

Transition planning follows the same process that you and your child's education team developed to determine an individualized education program. However, the plan for an older student identifies community involvement goals beyond secondary school. It concentrates on meaningful short-term activities that strengthen skills for employment, independent living, and community participation. The team writes these plans into an individualized written rehabilitation program (IWRP).

The plan also identifies the agencies responsible for school-community linkage. Because transition relies upon

various resources, the planning team may include representatives from the home, including your child, school, consumer groups, employment after leaving school, and rehabilitation, housing, recreational, and college services. Because resources vary from state to state, you may have to
encourage the transition team to be persistent in finding
the right services for your child.

The National Information Center for Children and
Youth with Disabilities recommends several ways your
child can become a participant in transition planning:

- Start transition planning during junior high school by
  seeking out career exploration activities. Talk with a
  school counselor about interests, capabilities, and the
  skills necessary for independent and supervised living
  arrangements. Participate in vocational assessment.
- Incorporate information about interests and capabilities
  into realistic preliminary decisions about possible ca-
  reers. Decide whether these career choices involve academic, vocational, or combination paths. Read books,
  attend career fairs, and visit people in the community to
  find out more about career options.
- Participate in transition planning during high school to
  define and redefine realistic options. Guide your child
  toward coursework that is required for entry into jobs,
  college, or trade school, depending upon his interests
  and skills. Ask about government programs that prepare
  students for training beyond high school. Explore part-
  time internships in which your teenager can work to gain
  experience in a specific industry.

Address gaps between desired career and residence
goals and skill level with extra coursework, counseling, and
home training activities and responsibilities. To practice
what he learned, have your child become involved in early

work experiences, such as job interviews, part-time employment, or volunteering. Encourage him to join social and recreational groups in the community. Meanwhile, increase your child's responsibilities at home for shopping, meal preparation, laundry, and cleaning. Make sure your child can use public transportation, make change, and ask for directions. Break these tasks into simple components to learn step by step. Practicing and learning the skills required for work is *prevocational training*.

Some teens want to pursue postsecondary education. Since schools are unaccustomed to students with Down syndrome going to college, you may need to rely on your own resources for planning. Identify the colleges, community vocational programs, and trade schools that offer the preferred career options. Begin making plans by the second year in high school. Write for catalogues, financial aid information and applications, and visit schools. Identify and have your child take any special tests, such as the PSAT (Preliminary Scholastic Aptitude Test) and SAT (Scholastic Aptitude Test), necessary for entry. Locate educational institutions that have special programs and living accommodations for students with special needs.

The law requires that transition planning begin by age 16. Many states start as early as 14. Once transition plans are set, they must be reviewed annually and revised as necessary. The reality is there are only a small number of children with Down syndrome who ever achieve total independence. The numbers are growing, however, with awareness of what these children can accomplish if given the opportunity. Still, many more attain self-reliance by living, working, and attending postsecondary education within supervised programs. Early planning is critical to ensure your child's smooth transition into the least restrictive community environment.

38

‰‰‰

THE WORLD OF WORK

E veryone has a right to contribute to the community through some type of work. A gratifying job improves an individual's perception of herself and her satisfaction with life. Studies confirm that securing and maintaining a job significantly enhances the quality of life for individuals with disabilities.

Maybe your child has sufficient skills to find employment with minimal assistance from a social service agency. Perhaps she requires specialized training or a supervised work environment. Whatever the situation, each individual, whether mildly or severely disabled, is entitled to meaningful and integrated employment in the community.

What Type of Job Should My Young Adult Have?
The same guidelines for defining your vocational goals apply to individuals with Down syndrome. Help your child consider her interests, skills, capabilities, and aptitudes. Select a job that your child will find satisfying and rewarding. Weigh factors for success and what is ultimately in her best interest.

Consider your child's competence in the following areas:

    attention span for a job
    safety habits
    personal hygiene
    transportation skills
    time concepts

motor skills
ability to follow directions
money concepts
dressing skills
job interview skills
work social skills

Don't let anyone limit your child's work choices because of Down syndrome. People with Down syndrome display a range of interests, capabilities, and aptitudes similar to those in the rest of the population. They should be offered a variety of jobs.

Where Can My Child Receive Vocational Assistance?

Even with the best transition program, your child may still need vocational guidance after graduation from school. The primary agency for such assistance is with Vocational Rehabilitation (VR).

Vocational rehabilitation is a cooperative federal-state network that helps eligible people with disabilities identify employment goals and locate jobs. The agency offers a variety of services, depending upon what is available locally. A counselor assesses your child's interests, capabilities, and limitations for employment and conducts job training, placement, and follow-up when appropriate. Counselors should be aware of up-to-date federally funded programs that provide money for on-the-job training and work-study programs.

To prove eligibility, your child must have a medical examination that determines physical or mental disability. The disability must be considered an obstacle to employment that can be remedied by existing vocational services. Eligibility examinations are free from Vocational Rehabilitation. However, the agency may require payment for any or all of the services provided thereafter.

143

Contact your local Vocational Rehabilitation office by looking in the telephone directory under state agencies for rehabilitation or vocational services. Each state has at least one Vocational Rehabilitation office, usually in the capital. Other avenues for assessment and training are the Association for Retarded Citizens, state employment offices, training programs covered by the Job Training Partnership Act (JTPA), and local colleges and universities that may have special programs for youths with disabilities.

What Type of Work Options Are Available?

The type of employment best suited to your child's needs depends upon the severity of her disability and the amount of support she requires to maintain a job. The federal government defines three general employment categories: competitive, supported, and sheltered employment.

Competitive employment is a full-time or part-time job in a mainstream work setting. The worker receives competitive wages and performs a job alongside nondisabled people. Rehabilitation agencies may provide limited prevocational training before securing the job and assistance with locating employment. Thereafter, the individual with disabilities receives the same supports as nondisabled coworkers.

Supported employment is competitive work in mainstreamed settings. This type of employment offers ongoing assistance to people with severe disabilities so they can perform their jobs. Support continues for as long as the worker needs assistance to learn, secure, and maintain the job.

Funding for support is guaranteed under the most recent amendments to the Rehabilitation Act and the Americans with Disabilities Act. Businesses that hire workers with disabilities also receive significant tax incentives.

144

Community agencies implement supported employment through a variety of models. With *individual placement*, a job coach provides one-on-one job training until the worker learns the tasks. Training and supervision are gradually reduced as the employer begins to monitor the worker.

The *enclave* model combines a mainstream work situation with small-group training and supervision by a human services professional. Workers with more severe disabilities benefit from an integrated work setting while receiving ongoing specialized support at the job site.

Some vocational agencies furnish mobile crews. *Mobile crews* include four to six individuals with severe disabilities who travel to various job sites and offer such services as groundskeeping or housecleaning. The crews are trained and supervised by a human services manager who oversees job standards.

Sheltered employment isolates individuals with disabilities from nondisabled employees. Depending upon skill level, someone with disabilities may be placed in a sheltered workshop, work activity center, or adult day-care program.

Sheltered workshops subcontract piecework tasks from community industries, such as packaging, assembling, sewing, or stuffing and collating. Everyone in the workshop performs the same task and is paid a minimum amount according to the number of items completed. There is no opportunity for advancement or choice of task.

Work activity centers and *adult day-care programs* may offer vocational or prevocational training, but participants work without pay, and the emphasis is on development of social, daily living, and recreational skills.

Sheltered employment was once the only community option for adults with Down syndrome. Times and trends have changed, however. Now more employers and vocational counselors realize that there is a new generation of young adults with all levels of disabilities who want and need the opportunity to work.

Today's disabled youth have been raised with more normalized life experiences than those who were sheltered at home or in institutions. Consequently, they have acquired more skills and have greater potential to perform more meaningful jobs, earn higher wages, and work side by side with nondisabled peers. They just need the chance!

39

LIVING ARRANGEMENTS

The movement toward providing mainstream experiences for people with Down syndrome extends to living arrangements as well. Children who are encouraged to make decisions and take risks expect to leave home eventually. Parents who champion their children's independence assume they will want to live elsewhere as an adult. When families reason this way, everyone understands that moving away from home is a natural consequence of adulthood.

Until recently, housing choices for adults with retardation were limited. Warehousing in a few state-run institutions and privately owned programs was common. Residents came from across the state, leaving their families and communities. Once inside the gates, they rarely interacted with people outside the protected community, and they seldom moved elsewhere.

Now community-based residential facilities have replaced many of these institutions. Creative communities are devising a spectrum of housing options for individuals with disabilities. They are acknowledging that some adults with Down syndrome may have the ability to live independently, and others have the right to live near their families.

Acceptance within some communities is sluggish, however, and financial support and program availability are sometimes lacking. Once again, you'll have to do your homework to ensure the appropriate setting for your adult child.

Residential Options

Residential programs and what they are called vary from community to community. Basically, programs differ in the amount of independence and community involvement they offer residents.

Intensive care facilities serve adults who are so severely retarded that they require 24-hour attendant care. Staff supervise toileting, eating, dressing, and other activities of daily living. Residents may attend day programs outside the home and be supervised during nonprogram hours, or they may receive therapy and skill training on-site.

Intensive care facilities can be large, secluded residences, smaller institutions or part of geriatric care facilities. Generally, smaller residences provide a more homelike atmosphere; however, your child may receive more diversified services in a larger facility. Try to avoid placement in a geriatric center, where residents sometimes receive inadequate care from staff inexperienced with mental retardation.

Group homes accommodate residents in existing community housing. The number varies depending upon state and village codes. Live-in staff coordinate resident goings and comings and supervise activities at home. Group homes differ in the amount of independence, privacy, and guidance that residents find and the shared responsibilities and rules they must follow. Families and professionals prefer this type of residence because it offers supervised living in a more normal setting.

Adult foster care, also called board-and-care homes or family care homes, involves placement of one to five adults with mental retardation in the care of an existing family. The goal is for the resident to become part of the family while continuing to develop living and working skills. Some parents think foster care indicates their failure as parents. However, foster care can be an effective setting for continuing the training begun at home and an important first step toward apartment living. On the negative side, some foster care providers are unfamiliar with mental retardation and may be overprotective.

Semi-independent apartments offer some of the most imaginative alternatives for adults with Down syndrome. Within a semi-independent setting, a staff person lives in a nearby apartment or with a small group of residents and is available for support on a regular or on-call basis. The number of roommates in an apartment and the number of apartments clustered near each other or in the same building vary. One advantage of semi-independent situations is the opportunity for the resident to prove competence for greater independence.

Independent living assumes the greatest risks for residents and their families. Independent living is for those working adults who can take care of their daily needs, handle the finances of running a home, travel to and from work, and manage their free time. Even with living independently, most adults with Down syndrome choose to live with roommates. Roommates share chores and support each other through challenging times.

Your child's transition team should provide housing resources. For further assistance, contact the state disabilities, rehabilitation, or human services department. Your child may qualify for housing through the U.S. Department of Housing and Urban Development, or you can contact the national organizations listed in Resources.

Decision Making

Before you begin your housing search consider these questions:

- How much supervision does my child require?
- Does my child want or need a roommate?
- Would my child do better in a large or smaller facility?
- Can he care for himself, cook, clean, shop, pay bills, and participate in community recreational activities?
- Does my son need housing that is tied into a work program, or does he still need prevocational skills?

One way to ensure that the program is acceptable is to include the future resident in the search. Visit various residences together. Both of you talk with staff, residents, and neighbors. Stay for a meal to observe firsthand what life is like. After your visit, ask yourselves the following questions:

- Does the amount of supervision suit my child's needs?
- Who is available in an emergency?
- Is housing located where friends and family can visit?
- Is the residence near transportation, public entertainment, and shopping?
- What is the residence like? How do the residents interact? What are its benefits and drawbacks?
- Does the setting meet basic physical needs for food, shelter, and ability to move about without architectural barriers?
- Does the living arrangement offer consultative support and employment, social, and decision-making opportunities?
- Can my child follow the house rules?
- Is the neighborhood safe?

Start your search early. Locating the best residence and the application process take time. You want to ensure that your family keeps control of the selection process. Seek housing placement before an emergency robs you of your ability to choose.

If you cannot find suitable local housing or waiting lists are too long, you may want to organize other parents to secure another residence. You will need a great deal of time and energy to raise funds, purchase a home, work with your village to change building codes, and urge local support. But it can be done—if you begin early.

40

~~~~~~

FINANCIAL
ASSISTANCE

Individuals with disabilities may receive financial assistance from state and federal government programs. This assistance comes primarily in the form of cash payments for living expenses and coverage for medical services, although other programs may be available.

States differ in the payment amounts and eligibility for these benefits. Even programs the state administers for the federal government are subject to local guidelines that change frequently. Contact the local offices of each program for the most up-to-date information.

Four major federally funded programs offer assistance to individuals with disabilities. *Supplemental Security Income (SSI)* is a public assistance program that issues monthly payments for food, shelter, and clothing to eligible individuals. The program covers people who are 65 or older, blind, or disabled. When disability is involved, children can receive benefits from SSI as well.

The Social Security Administration determines eligibility for SSI differently, depending upon whether your child is 18 years or older. Recent changes in the evaluation process allow more children under 18 to qualify for SSI benefits. To apply at the nearest Social Security office, you need the names and telephone numbers of people who can verify the disability, such as psychologist, doctors, or a vocational rehabilitation counselor. Bring your child's social security card, which you can get at any age from the local Social Security office, and birth certificate. Carry a family income statement also.

Parent income is not considered for someone 18 years or older to receive benefits. For SSI eligibility, adults should have little or no income, be diagnosed as medically disabled, and be unable to work or earn significant wages to live, which the government calls *substantial gainful activity*. The amount that government allows an individual to earn through substantial gainful activity and still receive SSI benefits changes with revised regulations.

Social Security Disability Insurance (SSDI) pays monthly benefits similar to SSI coverage. The difference is with eligibility considerations. SSDI benefits are for people who became disabled before age 22 but have at least one parent who worked a given amount of time under Social Security and is currently disabled, retired, or deceased. Payments continue after age 18 if the individual can prove that immediate changes are unlikely and the ability to work is limited. When applying for SSDI, be sure to bring family employment and financial records in addition to other information identifying your child's disability.

Your child may receive SSI and SSDI payments, although payments will probably be adjusted. If your adult child is unable to manage payments, Social Security will arrange for someone else, a close relative or legal designate, to receive and allocate the money as necessary.

In most states, people who meet the requirements for SSI are also eligible for *Medicaid* and food stamps. Medicaid provides monetary assistance for individuals whose income is too low to be able to pay for doctor, dental, and hospital bills. Someone is eligible for Medicaid if the family receives welfare payments, the applicant is over 65 or under 21, or the applicant is between 21 and 65 but disabled. The drawback is that Medicaid has limits on costs and frequently requires approval for services before they can be performed. Without prior approval, the agency may not pay.

Medicare is federal health insurance coverage that is not linked to financial need. Individuals are eligible for Medicare assistance if they are age 65 or older or have certain disabilities, including mental retardation. Medicare pays a portion of hospital and medical expenses that result from inpatient or home care services, including respite.

Another program, called *Qualified Medicare Beneficiary* (QMB), assists people who may or may not have Medicare and do not qualify for Medicaid but have insufficient funds to cover out-of-pocket medical expenses. With the QMB program, the state pays your Medicare premiums, deductibles, and other insurance costs.

Information about these programs is available from the local Social Security Administration office. In some states, the department of rehabilitation has a special division related to developmental disabilities that also handles eligibility for government-assisted programs.

When contacting these offices, prepare for repeated telephone calls, long lines, and delays in processing your application. For easier follow-up, record who you talk to when and what they told you. Dealing with these government offices and the confusing programs they administer can be frustrating.

41

~~~~~~

FINANCIAL AND ESTATE PLANNING

T he problem with planning for the future is that it forces families to face many difficult issues. For some, there is the disturbing realization that their child with Down syndrome may always be dependent. For others, there is the prospect of dealing with inevitable mortality. These issues are scary for parents and children alike. When contingency planning becomes a natural part of your overall planning activities, however, the process is much easier for everyone.

Planning for Today

Permanent disability can strain the most solvent family budget, especially when unexpected medical problems arise. Even the best health insurance has gaps in coverage. Therefore, prepare now for your child's unanticipated expenses.

Financial planners usually recommend that families supporting someone who is disabled set aside six months of cash for easy access. The money can be in a money market fund, bank, or other investments. However, the program must allow easy retrieval of funds in case you need them for treatment or therapy.

Another important consideration is holding adequate life, health, and disability insurance. Check that your insurance companies understand what Down syndrome is and is not. Many companies deny or cancel coverage because of outdated definitions that suggest Down syndrome is mental illness or a psychiatric problem, which they may not cover. If you have difficulty with biased insurers, ask your physician to intervene on your behalf.

Insurance is a reason to be more careful about switching jobs or moving to another state. Some workers have difficulty converting policies because of clauses that refer to preexisting conditions. You must inquire as part of the interview process. States vary in their definitions of disability and the types of assistance they offer. These differences may affect disability benefits. Before making a move, contact local organizations related to disabilities for resources concerning insurance options.

Planning for Tax Exemptions

Recent tax law changes redefined the range of eligible deductions you can take. Currently, medical expenses must exceed 7.5 percent of your adjusted gross income before you can claim deductions. However, you can now take deductions for more expenses related to your child's care, such as basic dependency care, programs prescribed by your doctor (camp or a workshop for you), the cost of building physical therapy adaptations, or transportation expenses to accompany your child for care. Your expenses must be reasonable, however, and supported by written prescriptions from physicians and therapists.

The U.S. Internal Revenue Service details other tax credits in Publication 503, *Child and Dependent Care Expenses*. Keep detailed records of any expenses throughout the year that you think might be valid, and let an accountant decide.

Planning Ahead

Planning ahead is a project that includes everyone in the family. Your family may need many discussions to sort out the answers to these questions about caring for someone with disabilities:

- What does the child with Down syndrome need now and later?
- What support does the community offer?
- How can we best plan for greater independence?
- Who will be responsible for finances and overall supervision of care?
- How can the responsibility be shared so siblings can maintain a normal life-style?

All these issues involve the primary question of competence. How capable is your child with Down syndrome to make everyday decisions and those that result in more serious consequences? Your child's competence will determine the strategies you plan for a more independent future.

One way to assist your adult child is to structure a life-style that limits the number of decisions to resolve. Arrange with a bank for automatic deposit of checks from government benefits and wages. Establish a program so that the bank automatically withdraws payment for rent, electricity, or other regular expenses. Open a joint bank account that requires two signatures, by your adult child with disabilities and a trusted family member or friend, to withdraw money.

For matters of health and safety, designate someone to confer with your adult child and authorize routine or more involved medical care. In the event that your child is incapable of making everyday welfare decisions, appoint a trustee to oversee financial affairs and monitor living and working arrangements. Document your child's medical, social, and financial services and how to contact them. Place the information in an accessible file for siblings and trustees.

Estate Planning

The best way to ensure that your wishes are carried out is to write a will. A *will* is a written legal statement of how you want finances and assets to be distributed among your children and, in this case, how you want the care of your adult child with disabilities managed. Furthermore, a will governs the distribution of your estate in a way that protects your child with disabilities from losing government benefits. Find a lawyer who is experienced with disability issues to help prepare your will.

To protect your child with disabilities and be fair to other siblings, you need to understand state laws that affect guardianship and disability benefits. The type of investments and estate you create can jeopardize your child's eligibility for Supplemental Security Income and government medical assistance. Therefore, devise a plan that limits the income and resources awarded in your child's name.

- Remove your child's name as beneficiary for insurance policies, pension funds, and retirement programs immediately. Although this may pain you, keep your child's name out of your will in terms of direct inheritance. Many states appropriate inheritances left to individuals who receive disability benefits. The money goes into a general fund that has no direct application to your child's care. Advise well-meaning friends and relatives *not* to leave your child direct monetary gifts, either.
- Provide for your child with disabilities by placing money into a trust fund that is specifically designated for services not covered by government programs. The money may go for recreation, extra education and rehabilitation, or the cost of an advocate—anything but the food, shelter, and clothing funded by SSI.

Select a guardian or trustee to administer the fund. If you have several children, you may want to appoint two guardians so they can divide responsibilities.

If your lawyer recommends that you formally disinherit your child with disabilities, explain that this is only a formality. Your child will receive an equal portion of the estate through a trust that safeguards other benefits.

The care of a child with disabilities is a family affair. By planning together, family members learn to understand each other better and feel more comfortable with decisions about their future.

42

~~~~~~

LETTING GO

Developing independence is a lifelong process that leads all children into adulthood. The course can be smooth or rocky. However, your child with Down syndrome may have worked harder and longer, found everyday challenges more stressful, and encountered more emotional ups and downs than other children you know.

To ease your child's way, you invested considerable time and effort in providing experiences she may not have gotten on her own. You allowed her to test the world by failing, trying again, and succeeding. As your child learned about life, she gained the foundation for living and working on her own.

You planned that each of your children eventually leave home when they were ready. Now is the time for you to let go of your adult with disabilities, too.

Think of Your Adult with Down Syndrome as Independent

Many parents have difficulty viewing their child as an independent adult, no matter how capable the person. When you add Down syndrome, there is a greater tendency for parents to assume that the child will always be dependent.

One physician explains that these feelings come from the lifelong tension involved in raising a child with a disability. Pulling the parent one way is the desire to make life easier for the child while wishing the disability away.

Pulling in another direction is the striving to accept the person as she is. Once your child is in a position to act on her own, however, she needs the encouragement to seek a life independent of the family.

Treat Your Child as a Competent Human Being

Self-confidence is critical to success at independent living. Foster your child's self-sufficiency to live on her own by the following actions:

- Promote your child's assertive behavior.
- Recognize efforts toward a goal as well as the final product and accomplishment.
- Show that you value your child's opinions and ideas.
- Champion your child's ability to practice coping skills.
- Give your child time to adjust to being away without your interference.

Monitor Your Adult Child's Successes

Even though your child is living on her own, someone may still need to monitor that her programs are accomplishing what they claim to do. Is the community living arrangement providing the basic food, clothing, and shelter your child requires? Does your child seem happy there? Is she participating in community and housing activities? Does her work seem fulfilling?

Talk with your child. If there is a problem, contact the staff person where she lives. If you don't get answers, press the social service agency that was responsible for the community and work placements. Your child has a right to a realistic community placement that suits her capabilities and makes her happy.

Remember, You Are Still a Family

Letting go means accepting that you have a different relationship with your adult child. This relationship allows you to support each other as adults and respect each other's opinions and decisions. It means that even though you have a life apart from each other now, you can still enjoy being together as a loving family.

Keep regular contact with all your adult children, by telephone, writing, or visits. Encourage your children to interact with each other without you. Spend holidays together, and go on outings together as you normally choose to do. Letting go changes everyone's life-style—yours, your child with Down syndrome, and your other children's. As you adjust to your new lives, you discover that you still enjoy each others' company as a family. You've all earned this right!

QUESTIONS AND ANSWERS

Is something wrong with us for having a child with Down syndrome?

The incident during conception that caused the embryo to have an extra chromosome can happen in any egg or sperm cell. There was nothing either of you did or didn't do to make this happen.

Where can we locate information and a support group of other parents facing similar concerns?

Many national, state, and local groups can help you. Good places to start are with the National Down Syndrome Congress, the National Down Syndrome Society, the Association of Retarded Citizens, and the National Information Center for Children and Youth with Disabilities, which provides lists of resources by state. You can also seek assistance through your local school district, hospital, and university.

What type of life-style can I expect for my child with Down syndrome?

Expect to include your child with Down syndrome in most of your family's activities. Your child will walk, talk, take care of daily living skills, go to school, and enjoy a similar range of interests as other children. Although an adult with Down syndrome may always need some supervision, you can expect your child eventually to live and work outside your home and have a social life. A new generation of children born with Down syndrome is growing up with more mainstream opportunities. With more normalized experiences, these children may exceed previous expectations for independent achievement.

Will my child with Down syndrome develop at a certain rate?

Healthy children vary in their rates of development, and so do children with Down syndrome. Your child may progress at a steady pace or reach occasional plateaus. However, Down syndrome may affect your child by slowing the overall rate of development. Early and continuous stimulation will improve general development and help increase capacity in the areas changed by Down syndrome.

Will my child be retarded?

Almost all children with Down syndrome have some degree of retardation, a slower rate of development. The degree varies widely, from mild to moderate to severe. Most children with Down syndrome fall into the mild to moderate range, with a few achieving nearly normal levels. There is no way to predict any retardation with certainty.

Will my child learn toileting skills?

Almost all children with Down syndrome become toilet trained. You can achieve the greatest success with the least amount of frustration by waiting until your child has the bladder control, physical readiness, and language development to be trained. Signs of bladder control include urinating a great deal at one time rather than frequent dribbling, staying dry for hours, and facial or postural indications that your child recognizes the need to urinate. Physical readiness involves the finger and hand coordination to pick up objects and the ability to walk to another room. Your child also needs enough language to follow a single simple command and to imitate movements. Since there may be a slower rate of development, wait until your child is ready to be toilet trained.

Will my child be able to read?

Many children with Down syndrome learn to read, most often at a primary level. A few children achieve reading levels that allow them to complete mainstream high school and college courses. What is more important than reading level, however, is the usefulness of the reading your child learns.

If I have one child with Down syndrome, am I or my children more prone to having another child with the condition?

Yes. The possibility of having a child with Down syndrome increases if Down syndrome is in your family or the woman is over age 35 and the man is over age 50. To determine your chances, talk with a genetic counselor and recommend that your children do the same when they are ready to have a baby. If you are concerned about another pregnancy, you can arrange for the woman to be tested during the fourth month by amniocentesis or earlier by one of the newer, less intrusive blood tests.

165

GLOSSARY

Adaptive physical education gym activities adapted to the capabilities of individuals with disabilities.

Adult day-care program nonwork setting that provides developmental and social activities for adults unable to maintain employment.

Adult foster care placement of one to five adults with disabilities in the care of an existing family.

Alpha-fetoprotein (AFP) a protein produced in a fetus's liver.

Alzheimer disease a disorder that causes steady deterioration in overall brain function.

Americans with Disabilities Act of 1990, Public Law 101-336 legislation that entitles people with disabilities to equal rights in employment, housing, transportation, state and local government services, and telecommunications.

Amniocentesis test at 16 to 18 weeks of pregnancy for determining genetic irregularities in which a needle is inserted through the abdomen into the uterus to draw amniotic fluid for analysis of the unborn child.

Amniotic fluid protective liquid that surrounds the fetus.

Assessment process of gathering and using information about how a child develops to determine what assistance is needed.

Assistive technology any item, equipment, or system that maintains or improves functioning for individuals with disabilities.

Atlantoaxial instability   poor muscle tone of the top two vertebrae of the spinal column that creates weak head control.

Audiologist   trained clinician who tests for hearing loss.

Barts triple test   newer blood test for women 16 weeks pregnant that tests for elevated levels of chemicals that indicate Down syndrome.

Behavior modification   a strategy for molding actions with positive reinforcement.

Best Buddies   organization that matches college students with teens and young adults who have mild to moderate retardation for the purpose of friendship.

Bonding   the process of forming a close attachment with a baby.

Cardiac catheterization   test that views inside the heart by inserting a slender, flexible tube into a vein going to the heart.

Cardiologist   medical doctor who specializes in heart disease.

Case manager   individual with a background in early childhood education who coordinates early intervention services for the child between home and the program.

Cataracts   condition that causes a film to grow over the lens of the eye and cloud vision.

Children's Justice Act of 1988, Public Law 99-401   legislation that authorizes state funding to develop and establish affordable respite care programs and crisis nurseries.

Children with Disability Temporary Care Reauthorization Act of 1989   amendment to the Children's Justice Act of 1988 authorizing funding for respite care programs.

Chorionic villus sampling (CVS)   test taken between 8 and 11 weeks of pregnancy to check for Down syndrome that involves removing cells from the developing placenta through the cervix.

Chromosomes parts of body cells that house the microscopic rods called genes that determine characteristics.

Circle of Friends program concept in which mainstream classmates take responsibility for befriending a child with disabilities.

Cognition mental skills of storing and processing general information to think, reason, and solve problems.

Communication skills development of speech and language.

Community services public and private organizations that provide human services.

Competitive employment full-time or part-time job in a mainstreamed work setting that is maintained without social service support.

Crossed eyes vision problem in which one or both eyes look inward.

Development orderly process of growth and learning that results from the interaction between an individual's inborn abilities and the environment.

Developmental scales checklists that measure a young child's progress.

Due process legal principles and practices that ensure that every person is treated fairly.

Early childhood specialist professional who is trained in the development of young children.

Early intervention programs services for infants and toddlers that identify and treat problems or delays.

Ear tubes tiny tubes inserted into the eardrum that allow fluid to drain and the ear to clear.

Education of the Handicapped Act of 1975, Public Law 94-142 legislation that guarantees free public schooling for children with handicaps.

Electrocardiogram recording of electrical impulses of the heart.

Enclave work model that combines a mainstream work situation with small-group training and supervision by a human service professional.

Evaluation process of gathering information about a child's total development.

Expressive language ability to use words, symbols, and gestures to communicate with others.

Eye-hand coordination integration of eye and hand movements.

Farsightedness vision problem in which the eye clearly differentiates only objects that are far away.

Fine motor development formation of small motor skills.

Gastrointestinal tract path that food follows through and out of the body.

Genes message center in each body cell that regulates individual traits of growth, development, and characteristics.

Geneticist scientist trained in the study of human genetics.

Gross motor development formation of large motor skills.

Group homes existing community housing with live-in supervisory staff that accommodates a given number of residents with disabilities.

Hearing officer impartial state-appointed person who hears both positions during a due process hearing and makes a determination.

Heart failure a condition in which the heart cannot pump enough blood to meet its needs.

Heart murmur abnormal sound of blood flow through the heart.

Human genetics study of the basic makeup of the body.

Hyperthyroidism a condition in which the thyroid gland produces too much hormone.

Hypothyroidism a condition in which the thyroid gland produces too little hormone.

Independent living residence for working adults who can manage all aspects of life without support.

Individual Education Program (IEP) a written statement of special education and related services a child will receive in school.

Individual Family Service Plan (IFSP) a written statement describing services a young child and family will receive from an early intervention program and how these services will be evaluated.

Individual placement supported employment through one-on-one job training with ongoing job supervision from an outside coach.

Individual Written Rehabilitation Plan (IWRP) written transition plan to identify necessary skills and agencies for school-community linkage to prepare students for adjustment into the mainstream community after secondary school.

Intelligence Quotient (IQ) computation made by comparing standardized test scores against national norms.

Intensive care facility residence that serves adults who are so severely retarded that they require 24-hour attendant care.

Intravenous (IV) tubes flexible tubes usually inserted into a vein in the arm for feeding and dispensing medicine.

Least Restrictive Environment (LRE) education term designated by law to mean the setting most integrated with nonhandicapped children.

Ligaments fibrous tissue surrounding bones.

Mainstreaming teaching children with disabilities in classrooms with nondisabled peers.

Medicaid federal and state program of health care assistance for individuals who are disabled or needy and meet particular criteria.

170

Medicare federal health insurance coverage that is not linked to financial aid.

Mental retardation slower rate of development.

Mobile crews four to six individuals with severe disabilities who offer a variety of services to employers as a team and are supervised by human services personnel.

Mosaicism type of Down syndrome that results when some cells have 46 chromosomes and some have 47.

Multidisciplinary team education professionals from different disciplines who appraise a child's functional level and progress.

Nearsightedness a vision problem in which the eye clearly differentiates only close objects.

Neonatal intensive care isolated area within a hospital for infants needing close supervision by trained medical staff.

Occupational therapist professional who focuses on physical skills that aid activities of daily living.

Otolaryngologist medical doctor who investigates diseases of the ear, nose, and throat.

Pediatrician physician who specializes in treating a child's overall development.

Pediatric nurse early intervention team professional concerned with health-related issues that interfere with development.

Physical therapist professional who helps bodies move better by improving use of bones, muscles, and joints.

Placenta sac that protects the fetus.

Positive reinforcement rewards for appropriate behavior that increase the likelihood of its recurrence.

Prevocational training specific instruction in tasks and skills necessary for employment.

Private organizations agencies offering a range of services for a small fee or on a sliding scale.

Psychologist professional who evaluates mental and emotional development.

Public organizations programs administered through federal, state, or county government and funded largely by tax dollars.

Qualified Medicare Beneficiary (QMB) federal program that assists people who cannot cover medical expenses.

Receptive language facility to understand words, symbols, and gestures.

Rehabilitation Act of 1973, Public Law 93-112 first legislation that mandated public programs to create opportunities for individuals with disabilities or lose funding.

Resource room separate classroom for full-time or part-time instruction by a special education teacher whose activities support children with special needs and their regular education teachers.

Respite care rest from caring for someone who has a disability.

Self-help skills activities of daily living involved in self-care.

Semi-independent apartments residence for adults with disabilities that is near a staff person for support.

Sensorimotor skills all large and small muscle movements and visual coordination of these motions.

Sheltered employment jobs that isolate individuals with disabilities from nondisabled employees.

Sheltered workshop employment setting in which workers perform industrial subcontracting piecework tasks in a location separate from nondisabled works.

Social and emotional skills sense of self and ability to interact appropriately with others that leads to total well-being.

Social Security Disability Insurance (SSDI) federal program offering benefit payments for applicants under 22 with at least one parent who worked under Social Security and is currently disabled, retired, or deceased.

Social worker professional who provides emotional support to children and families in stress.

Special education services provided by local school districts for children who have disabilities.

Special education teacher educator trained to work with children who have disabilities and consult with parents and regular education teachers.

Speech and language pathologist clinician who evaluates hearing and devises activities to improve mouth and facial muscles for eating, sound production, and communication.

Standardized tests measurement of intelligence based on the assessment of thinking skills applied to general knowledge and compared against norms of other people of the same age.

Substantial gainful activity government term for the ability to earn significant wages to live.

Supplemental Security Income (SSI) public assistance program that assures monthly payments for food, shelter, and clothing to eligible individuals.

Supported employment competitive work in a mainstreamed setting that offers ongoing support to adults with disabilities.

Task analysis breaking a task into understandable components to teach one step at a time.

Technology-Related Assistance for Individuals with Disabilities Act of 1988, Public Law 100-407 legislation that guarantees access to items, equipment, or systems that can maintain or improve a child's functioning.

Thyroid gland gland that produces hormones that are essential to control the nervous system.

Total communication combining manual signs with spoken language for communication.

173

Transition planning identification of community involvement goals and activities for a student beyond secondary school.

Translocation type of Down syndrome in which the child has 46 chromosomes, but one pair has a broken portion that attaches to another chromosome.

Trisomy 21 error in cell division that results in an extra cell in chromosome 21, which causes Down syndrome.

Ultrasound sound wave test that shows a visual picture of the internal organs.

Vertebrae the bones of the spine.

Vocational Rehabilitation national network of coordinated federal and state agencies that evaluate and locate jobs for eligible adults with disabilities.

Will written legal statement of how you want finances and assets distributed among your heirs after your death.

Work activity center prevocational work setting that offers skill training in social skills and activities of daily living.

ACTIVITIES TO PROMOTE YOUR BABY'S DEVELOPMENT*

Communication, Cognition, and Self-Awareness Activities

- Talk constantly as you dress, feed, and play with your baby. Sing songs, and recite nursery rhymes and finger-plays.
- Call your baby by name often so he learns to respond. Use his name in songs and rhymes.
- Provide different sounds to listen to, such as rattles, music boxes, a radio, squeak toys, a ticking clock, or bells.
- Make a wrist rattle by tying a piece of string between a rattle or bell and a piece of Velcro that is either fastened around your baby's wrist or sewn to your baby's sleeve.
- Place apple butter or jelly on your baby's lips and inside the cheeks to lick off and strengthen tongue muscles. Peanut butter on the roof of the mouth works the same way.

* Check with your pediatrician or therapist to make sure the exercises are consistent with your child's developmental program.

- Touch your baby's tongue tip with an ice cube. When your baby reacts by pulling her tongue in, say, "Keep your tongue inside."
- Offer a pacifier to strengthen a weak sucking reflex.
- Wiggle your tongue or move your lips while facing your baby in an effort to have him imitate the movements.
- Echo your baby's playful sounds. Make a game of coughing, sneezing, or playing dog or train together.
- Place your baby in front of a mirror so she can talk to herself.
- Tape-record your baby's vocalizations. Place him in front of a mirror and play the tape. Play back the tape to see if it encourages him to talk to himself.
- Blow bubbles together.
- Play peekaboo, when you cover your face with your hands and then go out of sight for a second. Another version calls for you to place a scarf or blanket over your head and then your baby's. Peekaboo helps your baby understand that you can be out of sight and still return.
- Play hide-and-seek with your baby. To encourage sound localization, hide a radio with the sound turned up and have your baby find it.
- Cover your baby's favorite toy with a diaper or cloth. See if your baby will retrieve it.
- Drop an object into bathwater. See if your baby goes after it.
- Prepare a scrapbook or photograph album of familiar pictures to name. Begin reading together early. Books, catalogs, newspapers, and magazines provide endless pictures to talk about.
- Have your older baby point to body parts on a picture of himself.
- Tell your baby the names of things she is using. When she is able to repeat single words, extend the words to simple sentences, such as "This is a ball."

- Play listening games, like following one-step directions or listening on the telephone. Have your older baby differentiate between objects, such as "Give me the blue shoe," or "Where is your nose?"
- Encourage pretending games. Give your baby old hats, shoes, purses, and scarves for dressing up in front of a mirror. Have him put a stuffed animal to bed.
- Make a surprise box or bag filled with different objects. Have your child reach in and describe sizes, shapes, and textures. Can she guess what they are?

Sensorimotor Activities

- Sit on the floor, and place your baby across your leg to encourage head control. Hold your infant high at your shoulder to foster head control.
- Place your baby on her side to watch what goes on around her. Bolster her body with a pillow or rolled blanket or towel.
- Carry your baby in different positions to strengthen different muscles—cradled in your arms, upright on your shoulder, or football style cradled in one arm. Lie on your back, and lift your baby in the air to see your face from a different position.
- Place your hands close to your baby's shoulders when lifting him so his arms move forward. This helps him learn to bring his hands to the midpoint of his body and find his mouth.
- Lay your baby on her back, and place large objects on her chest. Encourage her to swat them.
- Hold your baby upright with his feet on the floor. Take away your support slightly so he starts to bear weight on his feet.
- Place your baby on her stomach with a stuffed animal in front of her to see if she will lift her head to see the face.

- Lay your baby on his stomach on a blanket. Pull the blanket slowly across the floor to encourage head control and balance.
- Rock your baby on a large beach ball to strengthen neck muscles (after she has some head control).
- Move a brightly colored object horizontally in front of your infant's eyes. Encourage him to track the object. Then move objects vertically.
- Wipe your infant's body parts gently with different textures, such as a towel, silken scarf, feather, or paintbrush.
- Place your baby on her back in the bathtub lined with a large beach towel and about two inches of water. Watch her practice kicking while she experiences the sound and feel of splashing.
- Gently exercise and massage your baby's arms and legs. Play bicycle with his legs, and move his arms up and down. Roll your baby from side to side gently.
- Assist your baby's attempts to roll over by placing her on an incline. Use her crib mattress on the floor with something to prop it up.
- Place a brightly colored mitten on his hands and different colors of socks on his feet so he can to watch them.
- Sew bells securely on your baby's feet to foster body awareness.
- Stick a piece of tape on your baby's toe, and let her pull it off. Alternate with a cotton ball between the toes.
- Prepare extra thick jello blocks for your baby to feed herself and practice her finger-thumb grasp.
- Tie one end of a ribbon onto a bagel and the other to the high chair. Have your baby pull in the ribbon.
- Stack several sizes of cans or boxes, and allow your baby to pull them apart.

- Hold your baby in your lap on a glider or chair swing, and rock to establish sitting balance.
- Have your baby imitate your body movements while you both face a mirror.
- Help your baby learn to creep by holding his forearms while he is in a kneeling position.
- Supply your baby with a large box, doll buggy, or shopping cart or sturdy chair to push when learning to walk.
- Give your baby one end of a scarf, and hold the other to give her confidence in walking.
- Place large sheets of paper or newspaper on a covered floor. Place a blob of shaving cream on the paper with a drop of food coloring, and let your older baby finger paint.
- Let your baby tear and rip old magazines and newspapers. Ask him to tear *big* and *little* shapes. As he becomes more skillful, ask him to tear actual shapes.
- Play group and individual games and sports, such as swimming, ball, and bicycle riding, once your baby can walk.

WHAT OTHERS WANT TO KNOW ABOUT YOUR CHILD

General Observations

- Is your child generally happy?
- What does your child prefer to do?
- What does your child dislike doing?
- How long can your child attend to an activity?
- Does your child's energy level vary during the day? Which are peak periods for attending and learning? Which are the worst times to introduce an activity? Does your child tire easily?
- What motivates your child? What would be a good reward for your child?
- Who motivates your child? Does your child have a favorite person or people?
- Is your child aware of surroundings and people?
- Does your child follow a routine?
- How does your child react to daily activities, such as eating, sleeping, bathing, and dressing?
- How does your child react to changes and new experiences?
- Does your child seem to hear and see adequately?
- Does your child prefer to play alone or with other children or adults?

Observing Your Baby (Birth to Age Two Years)
Communication

- What types of sounds does your child make? Do they vary or are they repeated on a given occasion? Do they vary with the occasion, such as when happy or uncomfortable?
- When do you hear these sounds?
- Which activities seem to trigger sounds?
- Does your child look at you when you speak or make sounds?
- Does your child respond to his or her name?
- Does your child try to imitate speech sounds or words you make?
- Can your child put words together to make simple sentences?

Sensorimotor

- Does your baby react differently to information presented visually, aurally, tactilely, or by motion, such as swinging or spinning? What is the response?
- Does your baby like to be touched and held? How do you know?
- Which position does your child prefer—back, side, stomach, upright, or sitting? Which position does your child prefer for resting?
- Do loud or strange sounds startle your baby? Does the child turn the head toward sounds?
- Does your child reach for objects?
- Can your child hold objects? How: with one or both hands?
- Does your child prefer one side of the body or hand over the other?
- How does your child position the body for different activities—resting, playing, and moving?
- Can your child lift the head, roll over, sit (with or without support), rock in a crawling position, crawl,

stand or walk, run, jump, or climb stairs (up and down)? Is there anything unusual about the way your child accomplishes these tasks?
- Does your child imitate movements?

Cognitive Learning
- Does your baby like to explore?
- How does your baby explore: with the mouth, fingers, whole hands, or whole body?
- What does your baby do when confronted with something new: a toy, a food, or a location?
- Does your baby learn better doing one thing at a time or alternating activities frequently?
- Where does your baby remain interested in an activity longer: on the floor, in the crib, in a chair, or in your arms?

Social and Emotional
- Does your baby reach out to you?
- Does your baby prefer to be left alone, be in viewing distance of someone, or be actively involved with another person?
- Does your baby seem alert?
- Is your child persistent?
- Does your child look for objects or people once they are out of view or reach?

Observing Your School-Age Child
Communication
- Does your child indicate *yes* and *no?*
- How does your child make needs known?
- Can your child imitate phrases or simple sentences?
- Does your child follow simple directions, such as "Come here," "Look at me," or "Give me the ball"?
- Does your child volunteer information or initiate conversation?

Sensorimotor
- Does your child seem to learn better when information is transmitted by seeing, hearing, or feeling?
- Does your child favor one hand for activities?
- Can your child turn handles?
- Can your child build a tower with blocks?
- Does your child use scissors, crayon, paintbrush, and pencil? What does your child do with these objects?
- Can your child copy simple shapes?
- How does your child throw a ball?
- Does your child have good balance?
- What does your child like to play on at the playground?
- Does your child have any unusual gross motor skills?

Cognitive Learning
- Does your child recognize or express basic concepts and qualities, such as up-down, hot-cold, and same-different?
- Can your child label or tell you the names of objects from the house and community?
- Which activities seem to hold your child's attention?
- What has your child learned recently?
- What is your child interested in learning?

Social and Emotional
- Does your child follow established rules?
- Can your child wait for turns?
- How does your child play with other children?
- Does your child have responsibilities within your family?
- Does your child have friends? How do they interact?
- What does your child like to do with free time?
- How does your child handle frustration?
- How do you reward your child?
- How do you deal with inappropriate behavior?
- How does your child act outside your home?

- Can your child win and lose graciously?
- Does your child understand and respect others' privacy and property?

Self-Help
- How does your child take care of toileting at home and in public places?
- Does your child eat independently with utensils and with acceptable table manners?
- Is your child aware of appropriate clothing for the weather and occasion?
- Can your child dress independently, fastening with zippers, buttons, snaps, laces, and hooks?
- Does your child participate in a washing, bathing, hair care, and toothbrushing routine?
- What household chores does your child complete?
- Is your child able to keep busy independently?
- Does your child stick with a task until completed?

SPECIAL NOTE FOR GRANDPARENTS

As a prospective grandparent you probably had your own set of hopes and dreams for a new baby in the family. You may have waited for a grandchild for a long time, and now you envision another generation. Maybe you view the occasion as a way to ease strained family relationships. When news of the birth includes Down syndrome, you are crushed.

Your reactions to the news may vary, and so will the responses of the baby's parents. Sometimes, tensions that were part of your relationship before the baby worsen under the pressure of trying to cope. Here are some suggestions to help you adjust to Down syndrome so you can help your children manage better:

- Allow yourself time to go through the same grieving process your children experience. You may not be the baby's parents, but you have been hurt deeply by the shock of a baby with Down syndrome. Cry. Get angry. Do whatever makes you feel better. Seek professional support when the grief becomes overwhelming. Then, seek ways to help your grandchild's parents.
- Locate current information about Down syndrome. Read hopeful material, such as this book. Accurate information may dispel some of the scary thoughts you had about the condition.

- Be a good listener for the baby's parents. Avoid platitudes and overbearing opinions. What the baby's parents need now is a nonjudgmental, sympathetic ear, possibly coupled with an understanding hug.

- Acknowledge that emotions are frayed, including yours. Let your children know you are available and want to be there for them. Offer guidance and support if requested. Then, back off. The baby's parents need to sort things out for themselves. This is their child.

- Communicate your feelings without trying to take over. Some children try to protect their parents from information. Tell your children you want to know what is happening and how you can help without being protected.

- Become involved with the grandchild who has Down syndrome. Play with the baby. Sing songs and tell stories to the baby just as you would with any grandchild. Help with infant stimulation exercises. Involvement will help you understand Down syndrome and feel more comfortable with a baby you may view as more delicate. Stay involved as the child matures. Along with the rest of the family, delight in the child's accomplishments. Give the baby an opportunity to win you over as any grandchild would. Discover that this youngster has a unique personality beyond Down syndrome.

- Be honest if you are uncomfortable dealing with the baby. Your children can help you learn how to handle the baby or find some other way you can support them.

- Visit another child with Down syndrome if you live geographically far from your grandchild. Fear of the unknown is much worse than knowing about what the disorder brings. See for yourself how someone with Down syndrome can lead a full life.

- Follow the same rules set by the child's parents. Avoid the trap of being too lenient because the child has a disability.
- Pay attention to all your grandchildren equally. Playing favorites hurts everyone. The grandchild who is singled out learns to expect special favors from everyone. Conversely, the other grandchildren feel left out and begin to resent the relative who receives all the attention. All children, with or without Down syndrome, have feelings and need their grandparents.
- Offer respite to your children. Suggest that you watch the baby, or hire a sitter for them so they can relax, be together uninterrupted, or run errands.
- Give your grandchild a chance. Accept that the baby will follow a different time frame for development. However, understand that the baby will develop. Celebrate milestones with the family, and enjoy being a grandparent.

SUGGESTED READING

General

McClurg, Eunice. *Your Down's Syndrome Child*. Garden City, NY: Doubleday & Company, 1986.

Pueschel, Siegfried, ed. *A Parent's Guide to Down Syndrome: Toward a Brighter Future*. Baltimore, MD: Brookes Publishing, 1990 (comprehensive reference).

Ross, Bette. *Our Special Child: A Guide to Successful Parenting of Handicapped Children*. New York: Walker and Company, 1981.

Seligman, Milton, and Benjamin, Rosalyn. *Ordinary Families, Special Children*. New York: Guilford Press, 1989.

Stray-Gundersen, Karen, ed. *Babies with Down Syndrome, A New Parent's Guide*. Kensington, MD: Woodbine House, 1986 (overview of early years).

Thompson, Charlotte. *Raising a Handicapped Child*. New York: William Morrow and Company, 1986.

Assessment Tools

Bailey, Donald, Jr. and Wolery, Mark. *Teaching Infants and Preschoolers with Handicaps*. Columbus, OH: Merrill Publishing Company, now Macmillan (Columbus OH 43216), 1984 (offers guidelines for assessment situations).

Wodrich, David. *Children's Psychological Testing: A Guide for Nonpsychologists*. Baltimore, MD: Paul H. Brookes Publishing Company, 1984 (reviews commonly used developmental scales and screening instruments).

Young Children

Good, Judy. *Breastfeeding the Baby with Down Syndrome.* La Leche International, 9616 Minneapolis Ave., P.O. Box 1209, Franklin Park, IL 60131-8209 (group also has hotline and group referral).

Hanson, Marci. *Teaching the Infant with Down Syndrome: A Guide for Parents and Professionals.* Austin, TX: Pro-Ed, 1987 (step-by-step manual for teaching skills to infants with Down syndrome).

Segal, Marilyn. *In Time with Love.* New York: Newmarket Press, 1988 (excellent for understanding development and providing activities parents can do with their disabled baby).

Siblings and Friends

Meyer, Donald, Vadasy, Patricia, and Fewell, Rebecca. *Living with a Brother or Sister with Special Needs.* Seattle, WA: University of Washington Press, 1985 (excellent, easy-to-understand book for siblings and parents).

Perske, Robert. *Circles of Friends.* Nashville: Abingdon Press, 1989 (excellent discussion of how to ensure individuals with disabilities build lasting friendships).

Education

Anderson, Winifred, and Chitwood, Stephen. *Negotiating the Special Education Maze.* Englewood Cliffs, NJ: Prentice-Hall, 1982.

Deppe, Philip. *The High-Risk Child: A Guide for Concerned Parents.* New York: Macmillan, 1981.

Sex Issues

Dayee, Frances. *Private Zone.* Edmonds, WA: Charles Franklin Press (teaching children skills to prevent sexual assault).

King County Rape Relief. "He Told Me Not to Tell." 305 South 43 St., Renton, WA: (parent's guide for talking with children about sexual abuse).

NCCAN Clearinghouse. *Child Sexual Abuse Prevention.* P.O. Box 1182, Washington, DC 20013 (tips for parents about discussing sexual abuse prevention).

Transition Planning

Marks, E., and Lewis, A. *Job Hunting for the Disabled.* Hauppauge, NY: Barron's Educational Series, 1983.

Scheiber, B., and Talpers, J. *Unlocking Potential: College and Other Choices for the Learning Disabled.* Bethesda, MD: Adler and Adler, 1987.

Magazines and Newsletters

"The ARC." Arlington, TX: Association for Retarded Citizens (association newsletter available to members that discusses issues related to retardation and advocacy).

"Dialect." 3031 Louise St., Saskatoon, Saskatchewan, S7J3L1, Canada (comprehensive bimonthly newsletter dealing with disabilities).

"Down Syndrome News." Park Ridge, IL: National Down Syndrome Congress (official congress newsletter published 10 times a year discussing issues and updated news about Down syndrome).

"Exceptional Parent." Boston, MA: Psy-Ed Corporation and University of Boston, School of Education (published eight times a year for parents of children with disabilities).

"Inclusion News." Centre for Integrated Education & Community, 24 Thome Crescent, Toronto, Ontario M6H 2S5, Canada (useful newsletter discussing all aspects of mainstreaming).

Assistive Technology

Apple Computer Company, Inc. and Trace Research and Development Center, University of Wisconsin in Madison. *Apple Computer Resources in Special Education.* Allen, TX: DLM Teaching Resources, 1989.

Hagen, Budd, and Hagen, Dolores. "Closing the Gap." P.O. Box 68, Henderson, MN 56044 (newsletter discussing microcomputers in special education; published bi-monthly).

Hagen, Dolores. *Microcomputer Resources Book for Special Education.* Reston, VA: Reston Publishing Company, 1984. (overview of computer-assisted technology for special education.)

For Young Readers

Bergman, Thomas. *We Laugh, We Love, We Cry, Children with Mental Retardation.* Milwaukee, WI: Gareth Stevens Childrens Books, 1989 (sensitive picture book about the daily life of a family that has two children with Down syndrome).

Dick, Jean. *The Facts About Mental and Emotional Disabilities.* Mankato MN: Crestwood House, 1988 (explains special needs to children in grades 1 through 5).

Litchfield, Ada. *Making Room for Uncle Joe.* Niles, IL: Albert Whitman & Company, 1984.

RESOURCES

Key:
+ referral/information
o local programs
x newsletter/publications
‡ funding source

Down Syndrome and Mental Retardation

National Association for
Retarded Citizens (ARC)
Suite 300, 500 E. Border St.
Arlington, TX 76010
(800) 433-5255 + o

National Down Syndrome
Congress
1800 Dempster
Park Ridge, IL 60068
(800) 232-6372 + o x

National Down Syndrome
Society
666 Broadway
New York, NY 10012
(800) 221-4602
(212) 460-0330 + x ‡

General Disabilities and Health Care

American Academy
of Pediatrics
141 Northwest Point Rd.
Elk Grove Village, IL

60009-0927
(800) 433-9016 + x

American Coalition of
Citizens with
Disabilities, Inc.
Suite 201
1200 15th St., NW
Washington, DC 20005 +

Easter Seal Society
70 E. Lake St.
Chicago, IL 60601
(312) 726-6200 + o x

ERIC Clearinghouse
on Handicapped
& Gifted Children
Council for Exceptional
Children (CEC)
1920 Association Dr.
Reston, VA 22091-1589
(703) 620-3660 + x

National Center for
Education in Maternal
and Child Health
38th & R Sts., NW
Washington, DC 20057
(202) 625-8400 + x

National Information
Center for Children and
Youth with Disabilities
(NICHCY)

P.O. Box 1492
Washington, DC 20013
(800) 999-5599 + x

Roeher Institute
Kinsmen Building
York University
4700 Keele St.
North York, Canada
(416) 661-9611 + o x

United Way of America
701 N. Fairfax St.
Alexandria, VA 22314-2145
(703) 836-7100 + o ‡

Rural and Military

American Council on
Rural Special Education
(ACRES) University of Utah
221 Milton Bennion Hall
Salt Lake City, UT 84112
(801) 585-5659 + o x

Department of Defense
Dependent Schools
Special Education
Coordinator
Suite 1500
225 Jefferson Davis Hwy.
Crystal Gateway 2
Alexandria, VA 22202
(703) 746-7867 + o

Specialized Training and
Military Parents (STOMP)
12208 Pacific Hwy., SW
Tacoma WA 98499
(206) 588-1741 +

Advocacy and Mainstreaming

The Disability Rights,
Education and Defense Fund
2212 6th St.
Berkeley, CA 94710
(510) 644-2555 +

Family Resource Center
on Disabilities
Room 900
20 E. Jackson Blvd.
Chicago, IL 60604
(312) 939-3513 + o x

The Mad Hatters
(theater group)
P.O. Box 2
Kalamazoo, MI 49005
(616) 385-5871 o

Planned Lifetime Advocacy
Network (PLAN)
104-3790 Canada Way
Burnaby British Columbia
V5G, 1G4, Canada + o

Technical Assistance to
Parent Programs (TAPP)
Federation for Children
with Special Needs
Suite 104
95 Berkeley St.
Boston, MA 02116
(617) 482-2915 + o

Support for Alternative Families

National Foster Parent
Association, Inc. (NFPA)
226 Kilts Fr.

193

Houston, TX 77024
(713) 1467-1850 + o x

Organization for United
Response (OURS)
Suite 203
3333 Highway 100, N
Minneapolis, MN 55422
(612) 535-4829 + o

Siblings

National Association of
Sibling Programs
The Sibling Support Project
Children's Hospital and
Medical Center
4800 Sand Point Way, NE
Seattle, WA 98105
(206) 368-4911
(United States, Canada and
United Kingdom) + o x

Sibling Information
Network
AJ Poppanikou Center on
Special Education and
Rehabilitation
991 Main St.
East Hartford, CT 06108
(203) 282-7050 + x

Assistive Technology

ABLEDATA
Springfield Center for
Independent Living
426 W. Jefferson
Springfield, IL 62702
(217) 523-2587 +

Compuply and Innotek
National Lekotek Centers

2100 Ridge Ave.
Evanston, IL 60201
(800) 366-PLAY + o x

Foundation for Technology
Access
1128 Solano Ave.
Albany, CA 94706
(800) 992-8111 + o

Talformaga Foundation
127 Central Park Ave.
Wilmette, IL 60091
(787) 853-8211 +

Sex Issues

Parents United
International, Inc.
232 E. Gish Rd.
San Jose, CA 95152
(408) 453-7611 + o

Behavior Management

Parents Anonymous
2230 Hawthorne Blvd.
Torrance, CA 90595
(800) 421-0353
(hotline and support for
stressed parents.) o

Legal Issues

Commission on Mental and
Physical Disabilities
American Bar Association
1800 M Street NW
Washington, DC 20036
(202) 331-2200 +

U.S. Department of Justice
Civil Rights Division

Coordination and Review
Section
Box 66118
Washington, DC 20035-6118
(202) 514-0310, voice
(202) 514-0381/83, TDD +

**Employment and Transition
Planning**

American Association of
University Affiliated
Programs for Persons with
Developmental Disabilities
(AAUAP)
8630 Fenton St., No. 410
Silver Spring, MD 20910-3803
+ x

Closer Look
Parents' Campaign for
Handicapped Children and
Youth
Box 1492
Washington, DC 20013 + o x

HEATH Resource Center
National Clearinghouse on
Postsecondary Education
for Individuals with
Disabilities
American Council on
Education
Suite 800
One DuPont Circle
Washington, DC 20036
(800) 544-3284 + x

Mainstream, Inc.
3 Bethesda Metro Center
Bethesda, MD 20814
(301) 654-2400 + o

President's Committee on
Employment of People with
Disabilities
Room 636,
1111 20th St., NW
Washington, DC 20036
(202) 653-5044 + x

**Respite Care and Crisis
Nurseries**

Access to Respite Care
and Help (ARCH)
Chapel Hill
Training Project
800 Eastowne Dr.
Chapel Hill, NC 27514
(919) 490-5577 + x

Texas Respite Resource
Network (TRRN)
P.O. Box 7330, Station A
San Antonio, TX 78207-3198
(512) 228-2794 + o x

Recreation

Best Buddies
1350 New York Ave., NW
Washington, DC 20005 + o

National Lekotek Center
2100 Ridge Ave.
Evanston, IL 60201
(800) 366-PLAY
(international network) + o x

Special Olympics
International
Suite 500
1350 New York Ave., NW
Washington, DC 20013-7111
(202) 628-3630 + o

Financial and Estate Planning

Internal Revenue
(800) 829-1040 or
(800) TAX-FORM + x

Internal Revenue Service
Consumer Information
Center
Department 92
Pueblo, CO 81009 + x

U.S. Department of Health
and Human Services
Social Security
Administration
6401 Security Blvd.
Baltimore, MD 21235 + x

INDEX